8-22-05
Stuart —
Spine made my "60 year
worth it — Not for much
— Best Wishes
Norma Mae Doty Taylor

Sixty Years in This Wicked World for Nuthin

By

Norma Mae Doty Taylor

authorHOUSE

1663 Liberty Drive, Suite 200
Bloomington, Indiana 47403
(800) 839-8640
www.AuthorHouse.com

© 2005 Norma Mae Doty Taylor. All Rights Reserved.

No part of this book may be reproduced, stored in a retrieval system, or transmitted by any means without the written permission of the author.

First published by AuthorHouse 06/10/05

ISBN: 1-4208-6417-3 (e)
ISBN: 1-4208-3962-4 (sc)
ISBN: 1-4208-4536-5 (dj)

Library of Congress Control Number: 2005903000

Printed in the United States of America
Bloomington, Indiana

This book is printed on acid-free paper.

Address of the author – 6369 N County Road 1050E, Mattoon IL 61938.

PREFACE

The idea for this book was conceived many years ago and would still be in the procrastination stage had it not been for encouragement of several and one person specifically.

A long newsy letter was written to enclose to a second cousin with each Christmas Greeting for many years. Responses would always be, "O, your letter was so good, so funny, and we read it over and over. We laughed and wondered how you find the words to describe everything the way you do. You are a born writer and you need to write a book." Each year Jean would be more insistent until finally the author started her first book.

In late August 2002, the writer stopped to visit with this special person. News that the book was well on its way was exciting to share. Mental notes were made as the reminiscing went back and forth from things that happened many years before. A few days later, the author sent some sample pages which included descriptive sentences they talked about.

The following is quoted from a letter of response dated September 10. "You got it! You got it!! TALENT!! The pages from the very beginning, which was a perfect way to start, are warm, funny, easy reading and I was drawn into each story. I felt like I was part of them, which in some I was of course, but to the person that wasn't, the stories would make them feel that way. We can all relate to the experiences in them in one way or another. I can't really say which page I liked the best because I loved every word, but I especially liked the Indiana Roof ones. They brought back some good times. It was always good clean fun.

I can't begin to tell you all the times I laughed out loud from the very first words. I read the pages over and over and I really did enjoy them a lot. With only the ten pages you sent me, I can't wait til your book comes out. I want to buy the first copy with you signing it of course. Also the next book, which has to be written and the third and fourth... As you can see, I am already a big fan.

I gave the pages to John (her husband) and went into the kitchen to do dishes. He read them twice and I heard him chuckling all the time. He liked the story about the car wheels being cross-eyed. He laughed and laughed. He said, "These pages are all good" and for John, that means Great!!

The poem about the cousins is, of course, right up there on top with the rest of the book!! I would go on and on about each story but I don't have a lot of time this morning. I am meeting some girls, (old women – ha ha) for lunch after our Bible Study."

The author read the letter from her cousin and humbly pondered the critique. The author valued the opinion of someone so talented as her cousin and respected her insight to recognize talent in others. She appreciated the encouragement.

Within a few weeks the author received shocking sad news that this vivacious cousin had suddenly passed away. The visitation and funeral reflected her talents and her life with displays of her own original oil paintings, the framed photo of the airplane she owned and flew, and the journal notes of her weekly Bible study. Truly remarkable tribute to Norma Jean Smith Sweet who did not "live sixty years in this world for nuthin!"

ACKNOWLEDGEMENTS

The page of acknowledgement will be the most difficult to write. The names mentioned in this book are only a few of the many people who have touched the life of the author. Each name and incident is written with love and the deepest of respect. It is the author's desire that those who find themselves in the book will accept her thanks for treasured moments. Others whose names are not written need be assured that if the author knows you, she thanks you for being a part of her life.

The experience of growing up on a little farm in Rural Brazil Indiana, attending the Vigo County Nevins Township school in Fontanet Indiana, working in Terre Haute Indiana before moving to Mattoon Illinois is a heritage the author treasures. She is proud to be the 9th generation of her Pilgrim grandfather Edward Doty who came on the Mayflower. She is equally proud of other names in her family lineage including a few: Creal, Burnett, Seymour, Cox, Beard, Sparks and Rohrer. She remembers her parents and grandparents, teachers, 4H leaders, class mates, the hundreds of people with whom she worked, church people and ministers, neighbors, and many friends.

Each story or incident is true and as exact as was told to her or remembered after many years. The author wrote this book for herself, for her family and friends and anyone who has the curiosity or desire to read it. The author wrote with the hope that it will be appreciated for its family history, for its poems, for its descriptive antidotes in the lives of those who influenced the 1945 high school junior girl. If any reader finds one line that causes a smile, a tear, or finds inspiration to become their best person, the author will have accomplished her purpose. If each reader will strive to make their corner of God's World brighter and feel His presence within themselves, their story will be enhanced, whether written or remembered. Perhaps they will pause and reflect and they will not have lived "Sixty Years in This World for Nuthin!"

SIXTY YEARS IN THIS WICKED WORLD FOR NUTHIN

The curtain was closed. There was noisy confusion with last minute preparations for the opening of the High School Junior Play. A few more minutes remained until the character introductions would begin.

All the play cast members were in costume and scripts in order for the prompters. The couch was slid a little more to the middle of the stage and all looked to be in order. After many hours of rehearsals and locating the stage props, the moment finally arrived. The show was ready. The junior class members sold tickets to relatives and neighbors for about a month before and there were tickets at the door. The chairs on the gym floor and the bleachers were crowded with students, moms and dads, brothers and sisters, aunts and uncles and cousins, grandmas and grandpas, teachers and people from the little community of Fontanet, Indiana.

The heavy velvet red curtain was opened about six feet and the class sponsor took her place at one side of the stage in front of the curtain. The muffled conversations of the audience quieted as she made the usual greeting to the crowd to thank everyone for coming and being supportive of the juniors and their class play.

The moment had arrived for the introduction of the play characters. The last to be introduced was the girl who portrayed the role of an elderly woman with white powdered, high-piled hair in a knot and wearing big horn-rimmed glasses sternly pulled down on the nose. She was dressed in a neat austere gray with white pin-striped skirt and jacket and frumpy old-woman's black flat shoes. She was really out of style for the typical high school junior in 1945. That character caught the attention of the audience when she stepped forward in the curtain opening. With one hand on a hip and a finger pointed, she loudly belted her line, "And I ain't lived sixty years in this wicked world for nuthin!" Her brother, who was ten years older, was sitting in the fourth row on a chair next to the aisle. He couldn't believe what he saw. He laughed so hard he nearly rolled to the floor. Roars of applause was the immediate reaction of the audience. The pace was set for the curtain to open wide for the class play to begin!

1945 TYPICAL BOBBY SOXER

The typical 1945 Fontanet high school junior girl didn't wear gray and white striped well below the knee, almost to the ankle skirt and jacket or black wide soled shoes. Full gathered flowered skirts, frilly blouses and black and white saddle oxford shoes with bobby sox would have been the normal attire. A year after graduation there was a class reunion picnic and the mod outfit for girls was a one-piece sleeveless blouse and pleated shorts with a separate wraparound skirt. In the heat of the day they took off the skirts to show their trendy shorts. Some of the boys thought it would be funny to roll up their pant legs and put the skirts on and didn't know Kodak pictures were taken for future reference.

At school the Home Ec teacher taught cooking, sewing and other homey skills. One year the girls bought one pattern and made dresses either the same or with variations. The style was a short set-in sleeve, princess fitted from the chest to midway of the hips and then the skirt was gathered on. Two girls used the same print material and others varied to either a stripe or different colors. Seeing these girls with their creations set them apart from the other classes and some could have established themselves in the world of fashion design. Sometimes there were flared dirndl or longer skirts that were gathered enough to wear a crinoline underskirt which added to the scenario of being a well-dressed jitterbugger.

The songs in that day were written to reflect the era of young men being in military uniforms overseas. Songs like "Don't Sit Under the Apple Tree With Anyone Else But Me Til I Come Marching Home," "Elmer's Tune," "Oh Johnny," and "In the Mood" were all good tunes for dancing with some for sentimental slow and others for fast dancing. The junior girl who played the sixty year old woman lived on a farm about a mile and half from Fontanet. She remembers her family having a really fine modern radio. If anyone was outside when one of the favorite tunes came on, the back door would open and someone would yell, "Elmer's Tune is on." If you weren't too far away and could run fast you only missed part of the first verse. It was before electricity on the farm. The radio cost $20 and had a dry battery about 6 inches by 6 inches by 18 inches long. It was smaller than the old fashioned radio that worked off a car battery. The old one had a big brass sound horn that took up the whole library table. After her grandma died some things were sold and her mother used twenty dollars to buy the new radio that had a long lasting battery and was much better than the old one that used a car battery that would go dead and had to be charged all the time. The dead battery would be put in a car that had to be pushed or pulled til it started and then drove enough for the generator to charge up the battery. Her dad liked baseball games and the news to hear what was going on overseas. Her mother liked the WLS Breakfast Club every morning and the Barn Dance with Lula Bell and Scotty on Saturday nights was a treat for all. Everyone liked The Hit Parade and couldn't wait to hear what the top songs would be. It was like a contest to see who could make a list with the best predictions. Those songs all became classics and popular for all ages known as the Big Band Era. Glenn Miller, Artie Shaw, Benny Goodman, Tommy and Jimmy Dorsey to name a few and often they made appearances in Terre Haute at the Armory and kids would clamor to be up front and danced hundreds of miles to the music. Lots of shoe soles were worn out having great fun.

SCHOOL DAYS, GOOD OLE GOLDEN SCHOOL DAYS

In Vigo County Indiana there were grade and high school city schools and each township had its own school. These township schools were usually three story brick and first through twelfth grades attended.

The township trustee was in charge of the schools. He did the hiring of teachers and secretaries and janitors. Teachers were "dedicated" and women teachers were single, not allowed to marry, so their devotion to the children and their teaching jobs would be foremost. The teachers were called Miss Mary, Miss Versa, Miss Wright, Miss Eileen, Miss Wells, Miss Jessie, Miss Thersa, etc. The teacher could decide if she would be called by her first name or her maiden name. In the late 30s or maybe the 1940s there were changes made, especially when the trustee married the fifth grade teacher and she was called Mrs. Archer. She remembers Mrs. Harkess and Mrs. Stitt, her fourth and sixth grade teachers.

The teachers were all good teachers and the kids got a good education. The teachers became friends of the students and the parents. The school was a hub of social activities. Basketball games, band and chorus concerts and class parties seemed to keep the small towns and surrounding rural areas closely knit. Everyone went to everything. The school busses were kept busy when reserved to take a class to Brazil or Terre Haute to the skating rinks. Sometimes the classes went only as a class and for special times when they could invite other students. Busses always went to the basketball games. High school kids knew everyone else in the other townships when they were the visitors at the games. Fontanet had about 141 in grades 9 through 12. The class of 1946 had 26 graduates. .

There was the junior play and a senior play. The plays were selected and tryouts for characters were a highlight of these years. Everyone that wanted a part got one and some preferred to be stagehands or prompters

The proms were in the gym and paid for by the juniors who did the decorating and provided music for dancing. Usually the decorations were strips of crepe paper (red and white school colors) draped from the top of the ceiling down the sides. Janitors were most helpful to have big ladders and they supervised kids to keep them from acting the fool and falling. The janitors stayed many years and did more than sweep the floors and keep the boilers fired. One Janitor, Mr. VanHook, had kids of his own of several ages and he pretty well knew what was on the minds of all the kids. He had a knack to know when one might have a problem and he always had a cheery greeting. Nothing unusual to see him walking in the hall with someone in a serious conversation.

A Fontanet senior boy asked a freshman girl to be his date for the prom. He was the brother of the girl's classmates and she had been to their house often to visit and stay overnight. She was excited to be going to the prom. Usually the prom was formal but this year it was just dressy. She had a navy blue faille jacket dress, very stylish with red piping on the jacket lapels. The white gardenia corsage made her confident she would look very appropriate for the gala occasion. The gym was decorated in the usual red and white crepe paper streamers and there was a band for dancing. Light refreshments were served but didn't satisfy hearty appetites. After the last dance most of the juniors, seniors and guests carpooled and went to either Brazil or Terre Haute. They would hit the usual hangouts for a burger and fries. Hills Snappy

Service was popular in Terre Haute and it was soon filled to capacity with Fontaneters celebrating after prom. When someone suggested they go to the bowling alley it was soon voted unanimously by the party with the freshman girl and the two other couples. The freshman farm girl became a little concerned when she realized how late she would be getting home. At two o'clock in the morning she was glad the car didn't backfire and the other kids were quiet so she could get in the house. The next morning her dad asked her about the evening. When he saw her enthusiasm of the prom and the dancing, the bowling and the burgers, he made her feel very much relieved. He said, "If it had been his prom with so much fun, he would have stayed out til daylight!" He was like that. He and the mother had instilled in their daughter the unspoken but understood expectancy of right and wrong, morals and immoral and a mutual respect. She knew what she should do and not do, and above all she knew she was trusted. Nothing would have caused her to knowingly break that trust.

The Ten Commandments were talked about often at home and explained with simple illustrations. Understanding these rules of the Bible from childhood was like a built-in yardstick. One could go to the left or right but there was a standard to return. God revealed the commandments to Moses and etched them with fire in stone. If someone can't name the ten, how do they know they are keeping them? 1) Thou shalt have none other gods before me 2) shalt not make any images nor bow down to them 3) shalt not take the name of the Lord thy God in vain, 4) keep the Sabbath Day to sanctify it – six days to do all labour 5) honor thy father and thy mother, 6) shalt not kill, 7) Neither shalt commit adultery, 8) neither shalt thou steal, 9) shalt not bear false witness, 10) neither shalt thou covet (desire) what is not thine. One could turn in the Bible to Deuteronomy

6 to read the chapter that lists and explains the Ten Commandments in entirety. The farm girl was taught that The Word has not changed but each generation in the World often struggles to make the laws of God relate to justify whims and actions of controversy. God's word is the same then and will remain the same.

Having no other God or image or bowing down sounds like something easy but actually whatever is put before God could be breaking the commandment and called sin. What we worship or comes between us and God could be an image. An evangelist said on a Sunday morning he drove by a man in his yard that was washing his car and polishing it and reminded him of the golden calf. What is the difference of polishing car or Baal that was keeping the man from being in church to worship God! Do those who use profanity realize it is blatantly breaking a commandment?

Keeping the Sabbath with no labour might puzzle the girl that grew up several years ago on the farm to live in today's society. Perhaps there was a time when food could be prepared the day before, the oxen could have a day of rest and the servants and no one had to travel or be a pilot or engineer, no power plants had to be manned, no hospitals with emergency rooms, no restaurants and the seventh day was a Sabbath to be kept. If one day a week is set aside with no labour, would the consequences be justified or would it be possible? A day to rest to reflect and make a change from the six days of labor and toil is a commandment still to be kept. Without specific times of rest set aside, to meditate, reflect and worship, the souls of God's children will run down. Thus the commandment of the Sabbath and the conditions thereof.

The controversy over the death penalty has many facets. The girl in the 1945 junior class play has thought hard and strong about it. She would want the case proved beyond any possible doubts of guilt and the system's appeals allowed. And when the crime is heinous, after five years at the most, the convicted one's life should be ended. She can't justify housing those in death row beyond a reasonable time for appeals. And without a death row for separate confinement, the most vile are mingled with the lesser offenders. If the judicial criminal system needs overhauling, it should be a first priority. The death penalty would be a reality for the offenders. Without a death penalty there would be no reason for the criminal to stop with one crime if the punishment is the same for multiple. The perpetrator could kidnap, mutilate, violate, torture or kill as many as possible before being apprehended. Life in prison for some desolate ones might be more appealing than having to fend for themselves. Shelter, food, medicine and clothing provided for life might not seem all bad. Headlines of a man 54 years old confesses to having killed 48 women, as nearly as he can remember. His sentence is life imprisonment. She wonders too if it is wrong to believe that God's commandment says Thou shalt not kill and that the convicted should be punished accordingly? Does an eye for an eye also justify killers be put to death. There are people with no homes living on streets days and hoping to find shelter at night, depending on soup lines through misfortunes of losing jobs or illness. Should not their needs be priority for monies spent rather than housing dangerous criminals? She believes providing for the needy rather than the comforts of the criminals who break into homes to harm the elderly or children or inflicts harm on any innocent person. The commandments were given by God to be taken seriously and human's interpretations need to be with prayerful discretion.

Shalt not commit adultery was commanded. The Bible fully explains God's perfect plan. Looking in a dictionary verifies the definition as simple as "the gift of cohabitation is reserved for a man and wife." When adultery is committed there is forgiveness as one realizes and needs forgiveness. God will forgive and forget like the woman at the well when Jesus said, "Be clean and sin no more."

Being forgiven from wrongdoing or transgression is the end of any guilt. Saved, or some might say converted, is the moment of realization and accepting a Savior to walk with to help prevent and overcome temptation. Prayer for guidance and daily forgiveness is the assurance for the turnaround or conversion that explains "being saved." Whatever the terminology, when it means the realization that a commandment has been broken, which is also sin, accepting the Son of God, Jesus, as Savior with something so simple as "forgive me and I accept."

Shalt not steal nor lie or be envious of what is not ours.

And another commandment added by the Son of God, "Love Thy Neighbor as Thyself"..... Those who don't love themselves, their neighbors will be short changed. Those who defile their bodies and minds with idleness, alcohol, drugs or anything in excess that separates them from the Love of God and rebel against God's wishes, their neighbors are to be pitied. The farm girl believes the kind of neighbor she is depends on how much she allows the love of God to flow through her. Love doesn't mean conceit or ego. Another Biblical lesson that bodies are temples of God, is a lesson the farm girl was taught.

She recognizes that there is much work to do, to learn the commandments, to keep the commandments and teach others. She believes that if all the pews in the churches were filled, there would be less crime. With less crime, some prisons could be converted to productive work areas and housing for homeless. She believes if the pews were filled, there would be more families staying together. She worries when there are first indications of a marriage breakdown, that there are not required conferences with ministers and elders to intervene as a first step. Any marital weakness when there are children, would be directed to council with clergy of the faith in which they were married. Sessions with teams of those who can help reunite parents would be mandatory. A system designed to enhance the marriage rather than destroy it, would keep families together. "Let no man put asunder what God has joined together," would be the ultimate goal, the expected normal. More families together would be less children deprived of parents who know and keep the commandments. The commandments that were etched in stone and revealed to Moses are the same then and now these many centuries later.

The Fontanet farm girl grew up to appreciate herself as a Child of God, and is humbled with God's grace for her shortcomings and grateful for prayer and forgiveness.

SMART KIDS OR TEEN SMART ALECS

The principal told the farm girl's mother in the 1940's that her daughter's class was one of the smartest group of kids and also the class that was the hardest to control. This class didn't hesitate to go against a rule. If they decided as a group that the rule was not the best for a specific situation or they couldn't see the logic or any harm, a better way was found.

That was the case one morning when the kids got to school and heard the dreadful news that a classmate had died in her home with diphtheria. The girl's parents had sent word to the school that the funeral would be at 10:30 that morning. Students couldn't be excused from school without parental permission. Kids in the little town who walked to school could have gone home for excuses. Country kids who rode busses couldn't get in touch with parents. The classmates were advised that the principal and class sponsor would represent the class and no kids would attend the funeral. Didn't take long for these sophomores at the time, to have a meeting and decide to break the rule. The whole class left school and walked the two miles to the funeral.

No one was allowed in the house because of the serious contagious diphtheria. The casket was open by a shut window that was facing the front porch. Family had all received antitoxins but they stayed inside because of the quarantine. Neighbors, friends, the principal and class sponsor and the entire class of 1946 were somber outside listening to the preacher who stood on the porch. The family smiled as they saw the classmates of their daughter, Marian. That might have been the last recorded case of Diphtheria in Vigo County.

Marian had a special friendship or school crush with classmate Merle Cress. After graduation it was so sad that Merle was found dead in a cornfield that summer. He was a tall, good looking boy and such a shock to hear what happened to him. It was heard he may have died of heat, or natural causes or some thought maybe he ate some green corn and was poisoned. Two classmates dead at ages 15 and 18.

A lot of kids were in the band. The school owned some instruments for those who didn't have or couldn't afford one. Kids started taking lessons by at least fifth grade. The band played for home games, county music festivals, assemblies and graduation. Band players in the class of 1946 asked if they could march out with their classmates at graduation. The teacher said emphatically, "No!" Miss Amberger wanted her band to sound its best for the processional in, for the special music, and for the recessional march out. Well, as the principal had told a parent, the class was hard to control. Several seniors were in the band and after some discussion they were united in opinion. They would be seated in the band before the other seniors marched in and would play the in-coming processional. As soon as the band played the Star Spangled Banner, The Voyager Overture and a Sousa march, the graduating seniors laid the instruments on their chairs and took their seat on stage. It was just after WWII and rationing, buying stamps to turn into War Bonds, and the class decided not to hire a speaker but do their own program. Seven of the ones with top grades wrote speeches and one girl, another Norma, sang a solo, My Task.

Mr. Pound was the county superintendent and he helped the principal, Mr. McNeil, give out the diplomas. The farm girl had the last speech and it went something like this: "This is my diploma. It is a symbol of public education upon which rests the perpetual being of the democratic form of government. It signifies the completion of the requirements for graduation from high school as determined by the State of Indiana. I believe that the effort I have made to obtain it will be rewarded with opportunities and achievements in life that could not otherwise be attained. I believe that these have been the formative years of my life and that this diploma will keep me ever mindful of: An obligation of obedience to my parents for their years of patient toil and sacrifice to provide opportunity for me; An obligation to my teachers for their efforts of guidance and wisdom in the fullest development of my physical and mental abilities; An obligation to my community for its faith in the support of the school which molds young men and women into the fullest realization of their individual and social value. I believe that my diploma is a master key to the treasure chest of memorable activities in fellowship and association with my fellow classmates all of whom have made valuable contributions to my social development. I believe that all of the powers I have developed have been the total influence of society and that it is my duty to use them, not alone for my individual gain, but for the betterment of mankind everywhere. What we have learned shall give us wisdom to guard and keep us safe against enemies. Our education will be a passport into the hearts and minds of free men, everywhere. May God be willing, I shall with all of my strengths and abilities abide with and keep all of these obligations that I have taken in the acceptance of my diploma." The farm girl held up her diploma and nodded her head to say Thank You that concluded the speeches.

When the ceremony was over, the graduating band players stayed on the stage. It became apparent that the band would play without them. The band seniors of 1946 marched out with their class. Within a few years and a little more maturity, each of these band players would have apologized for their rude behavior with the teacher who had taught them so much. They would have been sorry for disappointing her.

One instrument owned by the school was an old outdated upright instrument called an Eflat Alto horn. It was brass, dented and had no case. It was loaned to a ninth grade student who played a violin since third grade and was in the orchestra. The orchestra was changed to a band and the farm girl violin player had to switch. The alto horn music was treble clef same as her violin but had valves and she had to learn the fingering. Eflat horns mostly played the afterbeat but sometimes had melody solos. On a piece of music in 4/4 time it was like playing the "and" in counting 1 <u>and</u> 2 <u>and</u> 3 <u>and</u> 4 <u>and</u> or silent "play" silent <u>play</u>, silent <u>play</u>, silent <u>play</u>, silent <u>play</u>. The tubas played the beat and the Eflat horns played the afterbeat. In ¾ time the tubas played the first beat and the alto horns played the next two beats or the tubas playing the Upp and the altos the Paa Paa in melodious rhythm.

Some township band members were invited to play in county band concerts The township first and second-chair players all got to go, however when they were placed in chair positions in the county band, they were placed randomly in first, second, third or fourth chairs. The old beat-up Eflat alto player, who played first chair at Fontanet, was assigned a third chair position along with three others. Student Prince, or it might have been The Desert Song, was an overture to be played and it had a high E for an alto horn solo. Starting with the first of four first chairs of the alto horn section, each player was asked to play the high E. The first one tried and the note came out but with no quality. The next player had a shiny new horn and his wasn't much better and the next one couldn't get above a middle C. Coming down the line, the old beat-up horn had its try. The Fontanet junior girl set her lips tight after a deep breath from the diaphragm and the perfect mellow High E was hit and held for the required four counts. The honor to play the solo was won to prove that new shinier horns are not necessarily better.

Most evenings during World War II around 10 at night, the farm girl would take the old horn outside and play "Taps." She could make the notes crisp and mellow and people told her the horn could be heard several miles away in the quiet of the nights. It was a tribute to her brother and cousins and neighbors who were serving the U.S.A. overseas.

PREPARATION FOR THE COUNTY FAIR

4H Club was a part of the Fontanet school and the Agriculture and Home Economics teachers often continued through the summer having the Ag and Home Ec houses open for kids to learn about the projects. There was baking, sewing and canning basically for the girls. The first year of sewing was hemming tea towels. Most often muslin feed sacks were used. 4Hers carefully bleached the sacks and then took out the side seam stitches to make them flat. Ironing was an art that would make the sacks straight and a thread was pulled as a guide to cut the sacks in equal halves. The quarter inch seam was turned under and pressed before making the final hem. Often one hem was required with the sewing machine and the other with hand stitching. The tea towels were ironed to perfection and saved until the County Fair. Excitement was rampant at the Fair for the 4Hers to find the exhibits and see which color ribbon was on their project. Blue for first, Red for second, and White for third. To get the coveted Sweepstake Purple ribbon was a special award. Any ribbon would make these club members proud. As the 4Hers got older, the projects increased in difficulty from tea towels to aprons until self-designed outfits were made. Some of these 4Hers might be famous designers.

First year baking project would be muffins. Measure the wet ingredients of ¼ cup melted shortening or oil, 1 egg beaten, and a cup of milk. Sift together 2 cups flour, 2 teaspoons baking powder, ½ teaspoon salt and 2 tablespoons sugar. Add the dry ingredients all at once to the wet ingredients. Stir only enough to moisten. Fill greased muffin pans two-thirds full. Bake at 400 degree about 20 minutes. For variations, you could add 1 cup quick-cooking rolled oats in place of 1 cup of the flour. Another favorite was adding 1 cup of blueberries and reducing the milk to ¾ cup and increase sugar to ¼ cup. Cookies were probably next, cakes and then yeast. What an accomplishment to be promoted to making cinnamon rolls and cloverleaf rolls which were three little balls of dough baked in a muffin pan or monkey bread with balls of dough dipped in butter and sugar and cinnamon all pressed together in a loaf pan.

Canning was a popular project and a necessary one for the rural kids. Families had gardens and foods were preserved for their winter survival. Learning to use the tested methods as recommended by the U S Department of Agriculture Extension offices enticed 4Hers. Packing peach halves with the pit side up on the bottom of the jar and overlapping the halves pit side down allowed more fruit to the can and added beauty as well as making the filled jar more eye appealing. A syrup of sugar and water poured over the fruit before processing in a hot water bath or pressure cooker was the final touch for safe keeping. These jars were wrapped in layers of newspapers that protected the fruit from fading. The jars were washed and polished to look their best for judging at the Fair.

Developing skills, love of competition and winning ribbons kept most of these 4Hers in a club for about 9 years. Most kids wanted to join 4H as soon as they could when they were 9 years old and would stay until they were 18. During that time they become Junior Leaders and helped the younger ones. It was a lucky boy who married a 4Hgirl. Boys were in 4H too with projects of pigs, chickens, rabbits, cows and birdhouses. Both boys and girls did projects like rock collections, leaf notebooks and garden exhibits. Club meetings and Fairs were good for socializing and sometimes a 4H boy would marry a 4H girl from another township after meeting at the Fair. The motto for 4H Club is "To Make the Best Better." The theory of these words taught to always look for the good and then make improvements if necessary. Maybe the songwriter got the idea from this motto for "You Gotta Accentuate the Positive." When you look for the good you don't emphasize the negative.

Several years later the farm girl enjoyed 4H with her children. Linda excelled in yeast breads and won a trip to the Illinois State Fair to compete in the public speaking competition. Tracy had his rabbits and his favorites were the black and white Dutch ones. Both boys did bird houses and Steve built a heavy duty utility lamp on a stand. The Taylors had a double wren house and the lamp that were Coles county champion projects that went to the State Fair in Springfield.

On October 1967, there was a Letter to Editor to the Coles County Daily Times Courier in Charleston: "While sorting through newspapers to be discarded my interest was again drawn to the pictures and headlines of the recent Coles County Fair and the Illinois State Fair and the 4H members who exhibited their projects in competition. Pictures and stories of these 4Hers are refreshing diversion from the many other stories of restless, unsatisfied street mobs, arson, etc. I can't help wondering if any of these people caught up in these frequent disasters, have a 4H record either now or in the past. I truly doubt it.

In June, I was picking my daughter up, I happened to attend the last assembly session of State 4H Club Week. I was impressed with the approximately fourteen hundred high school age 4Hers who were representing counties in the state as they were gathered in the huge Assembly Hall in Champaign. During this week they had attended assemblies and classes, heard outstanding speakers from other states and some foreign countries, had gotten acquainted with dorm roommates and other delegates, had shared ideas and were inspired and asked to come home and share what they had learned with 4H members in their clubs. The climax of this assembly was the chorus of several (looked like maybe a hundred) with the young men dressed in white shirts and ties and the young ladies dressed in their pretty summer dresses. These 4Hers presented a concert of songs. The last line of their concert was a triumphant 'Lift up your voices ye creatures and praise the Lord.' Last week I hope many noticed the displays in the downtown store windows set up by the 4H clubs to be judged for cash prizes. These displays are worth seeing and it is hoped that a continuing interest in 4H will encourage parents to enroll their boys and girls in one of the many projects available. A young man who starts 4H at the age of 9 or 10 and cares for a calf or other livestock sets a goal for himself to be a winner and receives training to lose gracefully one year and then be determined to try harder the next. A girl with a goal in mind spends many hours in the kitchen or at a sewing machine developing skills and can be a blue ribbon winner with opportunities for state competition, there are many other rewarding experiences offered. Without a doubt these 4Hers will meet their adult obligations in our communities and government and industry, homemaking, etc. and have 'A Better World Through 4H.' I thank the newspapers for being interested in our Coles County activities such as the good publicity for the 4H clubs and other worthwhile groups. Good news on a local level can promote a trend toward a positive thinking and actions. Mrs. John F Taylor."

The 4-H Pledge was instilled in members forever: "I pledge my Head to clearer thinking, my Heart to greater loyalty, my Hands to larger service, and my Health to better living for my club, community and country."

4H teachers and leaders didn't live sixty years in this world for nuthin!

DEVELOPING SKILLS AND ENJOYING MUSIC

In 4H Club kids started young and stayed in as long as they could. You could join when age 9 and be in until you were 18. This philosophy carried over in about every other thing kids did. If they had a desire, talent, or skill they continued to develop any project they started. If it was gardening, they started when young enough to drop seeds, then learning to know the difference between the planted seed and a weed. If they made mistakes it was used to further the skills. One particularly hot day, the little ten-year old farm girl decided to help her dad by hoeing the strawberries. She thought she was doing like she had seen him do it. The row looked real good when she got the weeds out and dirt pushed around the plants until late afternoon when the strawberry plants were all wilted and laying splatted in the row. Didn't take her dad long to figure out what was wrong. His little helper had cut under the plants and dismantled the plants from their roots and the hot sun soon depleted the moisture in the leaves. Feeling very bad was punishment enough for the little daughter and she learned a very valuable lesson on the spot how to hoe and how not to hoe strawberries. That incident made her all the more determined to keep up with garden stuff. She didn't quit and she learned to correctly hoe and would teach gardening to her children some day.

If kids started playing an instrument, they didn't think about quitting just because they got tired of practicing. They had parents who could endure the squeaks of a misplaced bow on the violin, or ignored the struggle to make clear notes on a horn. If kids started in music, they stayed to be in the orchestra or band.

After graduation there were some not ready to give up their music. A band was formed. The Fontanet school was in Nevins Township. The group named itself the Nevins Novelteers. Novelteers was appropriate for the variety of music they played. The regulars included two trombone players, one trumpet, one tuba, a clarinet, baritone horn and an Eflat alto horn. The farm girl had to leave the old dented upright horn at school. She bought a used more modern version and it had a case. She paid $50.00 for the mellophone. The tuba player was the one who approached the graduated players to start the band. He was older, probably 32, and he had a 1940 Jeep station wagon. After a few trial and errors, everyone and everything finally found its place in the station wagon for music instruments, including the big bass tuba, and players to be transported to their playing engagements. Later at a circus there was an act where an outrageous number of people got in a very small car and it was unbelievable when five times the usual number of passengers got out. They probably had seen the Nevins Novelteers getting in and out of the Jeep station wagon.

According to the occasion determined what they wore. For dinners and meetings the girls had formals alike, one deep rose and the other a bright blue. The boys and the tuba player had light blue jackets to wear with navy blue pants. The band looked sharp as they seriously played their music. On other occasions they wore hodgepodgey outfits like a German Band. The trumpet player was the smallest in physique. He often wore two overcoats and a brown derby that made him look really dressed up and bigger. One trombone player wore a red plaid hunting-type cap that flopped over his ears instead of being snapped under his chin and made him look like he had hound dog ears. The Eflat horn player wore her dad's old pants and coat and felt hat so she would look like one of the boys.

The band played for the Farm Bureau meetings, many small town yearly festivals, and church picnics. Once in Indianapolis at the Hotel Severn the Farm Bureau had a state convention. The Jeep station wagon was parked in the alley at a back door. The players were in costume and unloading their instruments. They looked suspicious and the cops zoomed in behind them and there was much explanation needed to convince the officers they actually were getting their own instruments to play for the Farm Bureau convention. The Novelteers had a line of jokes they cracked between their songs. When the story of how they were nearly arrested behind the hotel in the alley was told to the audience, the girls thought, "well that is a new story and when did they think that up to add to the routine." Took some convincing for the girls to know it was a true story. The Novelteers were the originators of the joke: What do you get when you cross an owl with a goat? You got a hootenanny!

The years have faded some details of all the places the Nevins Novelteers played. One event remembered was at an annual community picnic, maybe Bowling Green Indiana, or Cory Indiana but some facts are still very keen. The tuba player was dressed like a frumpy woman in a big hat. The trumpet player wore a baby bonnet and had a big calf-size bottle. The tuba player pushed a big baby buggy with the small trumpet player in it... The other Novelteers, dressed like little kids, were whining and shoving each other like kids did and were pestering the tuba player to give them nickels to buy cotton candy. "She" was swatting at those "mean little kids" trying to get them to behave. This procession went all the way up the midway to the bandstand stage where they already had put their instruments. The crowd was very curious and it didn't take long for the benches around the bandstand to be full of festival goers and there were people standing up. There was lots of laughing and clapping through the hour-long performance.

The tuba player was a chicken farmer and he raised broilers and hens and sold eggs. He was clever. He devised a machine called a chickin picker. The Nevins Novelteers often took this contraption on the road along with a chicken in a wire crate. The dialogue started with telling about how the chickin picker worked. The chicken in the crate was put in the wood box that had a crank on it. A trombone player turned the crank knob. Everyone else put their arms on their hips and waved their elbows up and down and made sounds like a chicken squakin. Soon a door was opened on the chickin picker and out would come this chicken with no feathers. It was held by its feet and looked real made of rubber. This act got the intended laughs to entertain the crowd.

The theme song was Sleep Medley and included "Good Night Sweetheart" and "I'll See You in My Dreams." The two trombones added the smooth harmony that made this easy listening and probably left the audience wanting to hear more.

Kids who started music lessons stayed with it a long time and learned to appreciate music of all kinds. Lessons that lasted a lifetime.

Chicken farmers didn't live sixty years in this world for nuthin!

TEACHERS REMEMBERED

Teachers at Fontanet were the best possible. No one ever remembered having a bad one. Grade school teachers hovered their little students like mother hens to protect them from bigger students running in halls or skipping stairs. Miss Eileen stood at her classroom door and greeted her third graders as they were coming in from recess or in the morning. If she saw one in danger of a rambunkous sixth grader, she would snap her fingers. Her famous snaps could be heard to the next floor. It got attention and the bigger kids knew they were being watched. Teachers were on the playground to keep big kids from bullying little kids. They planned games that made kids run and jump. They made sure kids didn't leave the school ground or wonder down over the hill where there was supposed to be an old coal strip pit with deep water. Not many kids ever found out for sure what was over that big hill.

In Miss Eileen's third grade class a boy could not remember what 3 x 6 was. As much as the teacher would hold up the flash cards, he could never say the answer was 18. It was like he had a mental block. During reading classes instead of calling Harold by name she would say, "3 x 6 is 18 and it's your turn to read".... All the class learned that 3 x 6 was 18 and no one ever forgot it.

The classes were put in either Redbird or Bluebird sections and no one knew which was the slower class. Often you would see a Bluebird helping a Redbird in the coatroom or in the hall having fun with story assignments from the reading book or drilling one another on spelling words.

December 8, 1941, the day after Pearl Harbor was attacked, the teacher was crying when the students went to their Home Room. Miss Chandler had become Mrs. Brothers and her husband was called to immediate active duty to defend his country. She seemed old to the eighth grade students and she must have been about 24. She attended a school reunion in 1999 and said she and her husband enjoyed many years together. She looked wonderful and still played piano regularly for occasions and had performed in many countries. She was a music teacher at Fontanet.

Another teacher, Paul Turner, taught science. He got a discussion started in class one day when he said that brushing teeth was not necessary and caused teeth to wear out. Students riled up and soon participated in a heated discussion. Later they realized he said it to get their attention and also to sharpen the debate skills of the students.

There was a young and attractive teacher who taught typing, shorthand and bookkeeping. Miss Whitesell made the kids work hard and she developed the potential of each student. It was well known that Fontanet kids could get good jobs in offices without having to go to Business College. The Twentieth Century Bookkeeping book had ledger lessons using double entry ten columns. There was always homework and If the farm girl had a date that night she would be particularly careful to put the right figures in the debit or credit columns. At the bottom was the space for adding the columns. Sometimes the farm girl's mother and dad would do the addition and there weren't any adding machines or calculators... When she came home from the date, it was good to see the debits and credits balanced and off to bed she could be. If not she had to figure out what was wrong.

The senior stenography class was geared to teach advanced skills and improve words per minute in typing and shorthand. There were two boys and one girl in one class. A phonograph was used to play records and students took shorthand at various speeds of dictating. The classroom was off the main hall. and down another hall that had a large coatroom on one side. One morning the teacher left to do some errands and gave the three-member class a short assignment and asked them to study some shorthand abbreviations. They put on a record of Glenn Miller's "In The Mood" and one boy danced with the girl while the other boy stood at the door watching for the teacher to turn off the main hall to come down past the coatroom. They had done it successfully many times. The boy must not have been paying attention or the teacher walked softer so her high heels didn't click from a distance. They nearly got caught. They would have been in big trouble if the third floor window hadn't been open and the dancing boy was able to throw In The Mood out the window just in time to get back to his seat and steno notepad. They didn't try that again but it was good while it lasted. That is probably why the farm girl was a better dancer than she was stenographer.

Mr. Dean was the basketball coach. He was tall and thin with keen dark eyes. One year he had a championship team. Fontanet won the sectional with the B team after the A team fowled out. The Indiana State gym never had a more enthusiastic bunch of fans. One of these players, Don McDonald, went on to school at Indiana State and became a high school coach. Mr. Dean was the history teacher too. He made every student learn in his class. Everyone studied because they knew each one would have to answer a question every day in his class. Everyone was anxious to raise their hand to volunteer when they knew the answer to a question or they risked being called on when they didn't know the answer. For a welcome change from the grueling lessons, he would take one or two Fridays a month as a break from the history book, to have a Spelling Bee. Bees were probably not heard of in other high schools, but he made it fun and perfected the already good spellers.

In late July, there is a reunion for anyone who attended or taught at the Fontanet school. It was a thrill for the two girls who played in the Nevins Novelteers to be reunited after many years. They chatted and learned they both were "writers" and in 2003, Ruth Imogene Dowell had copies of her latest children's book, Mother Ruth's Rhymes. How pleased she was to autograph a copy for the former Fontanet Junior girl. Another classmate, Joe Koch, compiled a history of Nevins Township with pictures and stories and will autograph a copy for the farm girl in 2004. Perhaps the farm girl will autograph her book in 2005. The teachers molded and guided many talented students into successful adults.

Teachers didn't live sixty years in this world for nuthin!

FONTANET AFTER DUPONT POWDER MILL EXPLOSION

Fontanet was at one time a most thriving area on the Big Four railroad with 13 taverns and a DuPont powder mill that employed many people. Disaster struck in 1907 when there was an explosion that could be felt many miles away. Much property devastation and loss of life occurred. Fragments of metal were found in fields as far away as three miles for years afterwards as they would work their way to the surface in a field. The South School house about a mile away collapsed and the walls went out while the roof caved in. The farm girl remembers her mother telling that she was at the dictionary stand and she was thrown outside with one of the walls which probably saved her from injury. The teacher lost the use of one eye. People were in a daze. Farmers heard the explosion and went in their wagons toward Fontanet and many of these school kids were wandering along the road glad to see someone to pick them up to go home. The powder mill didn't rebuild and Fontanet's population dwindled. No one is sure how long it took for the number of 13 taverns to get down to 3.

The little train depot was repaired. The train stopped in Fontanet many years for passengers to get on and off and also for freight deliveries. Farmers took 5 and 10 gallon heavy metal cans of cream to the train depot to be picked up and taken to Terre Haute for Watkins Creamery. Butter was made from the cream. The cans were washed and taken to the Terre Haute station so the train could take them back to Fontanet on a daily basis. People met lots of people at the Depot. The farm girl's two little cousins, Imogene and Charles, lived in Mattoon Illinois. Once they came to visit and told everyone they had skated all the way from Mattoon to Fontanet. They really did do it. They roller skated in the aisles of the train that they rode. One day while his aunt was working in the garden, the nephew had stayed inside to have a snack. She had opened a quart of his favorite stuffed green mangoe peppers. Pretty soon he came outside and said, "Aunt Alice I don't think the mangoes were as good as they used to be." When she went in the house and looked on the kitchen table, the jar was empty.

GOOD OLE CARS

Transportation on the farm varied from walking, horseback, no cars, shared cars and three cars. There was a big shed open on one end and a closed corncrib on the west side. Whenever there was a car, it was kept in the shed. One such car was a bluish-green Auburn four door sedan. It was remembered as being a roomy comfortable good riding car. It also was a gas guzzler. It had the habit of having its battery run down and often had to be pushed out of the shed, down the driveway into the road and if it didn't start on the first little downhill knoll it was sure to start when it was pushed down the big hill. The Auburn was then turned around to go back up the hill and pick up any passengers who had been pushing so the joyride could begin or the necessary trip to town for shopping. Sometimes the seventeen-year old son could borrow it. He saw his dad hand him the last dollar he had many times and it would buy the gas to Terre Haute and the show tickets and maybe a pop for two.

Sometimes two families shared a car. The one with the best garage got to keep the car. One side open wasn't as good as having a door that slid on a track to close. One evening when the farm girl was a baby, she wasn't acting right and sorta went limp. Her dad ran down the road to get the shared car and rather than his wife and baby waiting for him, they ran behind him. The baby soon acted better but they went to Fontanet to the doctor's office anyway. Doctor Newlin said taking the baby out in the air was what it needed and running caused enough breeze for the baby to be revived. Just knowing that car was only about 1/8 mile away was comforting.

And when there was no car except one in a mile, everyone kept in touch with the man who had that car.

He and his wife usually went to Terre Haute at least once a month. If you asked early, maybe you could ride along. And they kept a list of what the ones in the neighborhood needed from the city. Mr. and Mrs. Sullivan were good as gold and never fretted at having to do the extra shopping. They didn't have any children so maybe that is why they had money enough for a car.

When financial situations improved so did the acquiring and ownership of cars. The farm girl's dad bought a 1931 Chevy and he loved that old car. When city relatives came to visit, there was one especially who didn't like to walk. He had a sleek, nile-green, rounded-look Nash that looked like a boat. Instead of parking at the road, or even in the driveway, Uncle Jesse preferred to drive thru the yard up to the front door. The car was full of people and kids, suitcases and sacks of flour and sugar which was a lot to carry far. One time after a lot of rain the Nash made it to the front door before it sank in the soft grass. The dad was sure proud to hook on and pull the new Nash out of the mud with his 1931 Chevy. When anyone's car wouldn't start, he would brag that his old car always run.

One time it was raining and it was Canasta night. Four or five couples regularly played at one another houses. The old Chevy had a leaky roof so while he drove, his wife held the umbrella over both of them. He was a peace-loving man and it was a good thing no one made any fun of this scene. You probably could have said something derogatory about this man's wife, not that anyone would, and it wouldn't have riled him as much as if you said something bad about his cars.

At the crossroad of the Rio Grande and the Rosedale pavement was a little town of Sandcut. At the filling station one day, there was a For Sale sign on a 1932

Chevy for a good price and the farm girl's dad bought it. Nothing better than having two good old cars. He found a way that the passenger seat and the back seat could be easily taken out and put back in. He did that on one of the Chevys that he drove to the Pennsylvania Railroad yards during WWII when there was a dire need for older men to work. A lot of men were in the military service or working in related factories producing airplane engines and ammunition. His daughter knew how to put the front passenger seat in and out. She put it in one time and invited a cute classmate to take a ride with her. With the front passenger seat in but the pin missing, when she let her foot off the clutch and revved the engine, the front seat lurched and the young man landed in the back seat. He probably didn't think it was as funny as she did because they never developed a friendship beyond a slight wave if they met in the hall at school.

Sometimes the driveway would get very soft and muddy and the cars made ruts. In the wintertime with the kitchen stove and the living room coal heater, there were more ashes and cinders than in the summer time. Spring freezing and thawing made the driveway its worst. The neighbor man in the first house down the road had a job at the Terre Haute Tribune Star. Clyde asked if he could borrow a car. His nice new truck had something wrong with it. The 1931 Chevy had just barely made it through the soft ruts and was pretty muddy but the dad was proud to loan his dependable car to someone whose newer vehicle wouldn't run. The passenger and back seats were taken out making space to haul the newspapers to various locations in the area for paper boys to pick up to deliver. No doubt the neighbor was glad when he could return the muddy Chevy and get back in his new shiny truck.

It was one of these old cars the 14 year old daughter learned to drive. It was handy for her to take seed to fields or dad's lunch and cold water. At still a much-too-young-age to drive, when her dad was too busy or tired, it was handy for him to send her to Fontanet to the feed store to pick up sacks of corn and middlins or sacks of chicken scratch. The front fenders were wide enough that the feed store man, Harley Rosser, could throw 50 or 100 pound sacks on the fenders and the feed rode just fine. She didn't make these trips without many instructions how to slow down before turning from one road to the other, stop and look real good before leaving the narrow gravel road to get on the Rio Grande pavement. She was warned to not look where she didn't want to go, which meant look straight down the road. And there was a busy railroad track. Cautioned to look good to see if the flashers were on, and to slow down and then shift into second gear and make sure you were in that gear before crossing. The moral of the story was to never shift gears in the middle of the tracks.

Her mother drove when she was younger and lived closer to Terre Haute. One day as the mother turned a corner and crossed the interurban tracks, the car door flew open and her young son went out onto the street. He wasn't hurt but after she got that car home, she never drove again. The daughter got to drive and take her mother to lots of places even to Terre Haute. About the only place her daughter could drive by herself was to Fontanet.

JOBS AFTER GRADUATION

When the farm girl graduated from high school, she got a job in Terre Haute. She rode the Turner bus line that started in Fontanet and stopped at Burnett and other little towns to Terre Haute. This was a great service and only cost two dollars for a weekly ticket. She worked at this job for 18 months and it was boring and not using the typing, shorthand and bookkeeping she had learned in school. Instead, all she did was take bundles of magazine subscriptions and make stacks of the various ones. Pathfinder magazine was one example. After sorting with her thumb, she put rubber bands around the stacks and put them in a folder for another department to give the Sales Managers their reports. There was a supervisor at a desk facing about six desks of workers in each department and there were about six departments on the whole floor. Payday lunch hours were interesting to see the supervisors who managed to be late. They would come in one at a time so everyone could see how many sacks they had from which of the department stores. The owners and managers had glass offices up front. If one worker did something wrong, instead of that one being reprimanded, the whole department was led by the supervisor to the front office where the door was shut but everyone could see. They didn't know if someone had forgotten to dot an i or if someone miscalculated a report. One of the managers was running for Mayor of Terre Haute. For months there were visitors from various walks of life invited to talk with this candidate. He greeted them all with big handshakes and big smiles and they left with him patting them on their back.

This boring job went from boring to more boring until one morning the farm girl just stayed home. And the next day she stayed home again until she was rather enjoying it. In about a week she saw an ad in the paper for someone in the Sorting Department.

There was an apple orchard three miles away from her parents' little farm. They heard apple pickers were needed... She went with her mom and dad, who knew the owner, to see about a job to make some extra money. The orchard owner was the Republican candidate for Mayor of Terre Haute. The owner greeted the mom and dad as they drove in and the mom introduced her daughter. She told Mr. Adams that her daughter had been working for the Democrat candidate for Mayor and thought she would like to work for the Republican. The owner thought that was a coincidental big-time story and he laughed and assigned some trees for them to start picking. Later in the afternoon, he sent word for them to stop by the house before they went home. He had gone to Terre Haute to have lunch with some business friends. A Commercial Solvents Corporation executive was there who just happened to mention there was an opening for a secretary. What a coincidence that the owner of the apple orchard had just met a certain young lady with office experience that probably would work out just fine for the executive. He made an appointment for an interview.

The farm girl's mother always went to Terre Haute in the car with her daughter. That morning they even did the trendy mother/daughter dress alike. Their dresses were latest fashion in a black and white print with a black faille peplum just below the waist, dual-striking outfits. The mother and daughter found the building for the interview and walked in together. Probably most job searchers went alone and not with their mothers and dressed alike. One man at a desk must have summed up the situation. He went to the mother and invited her to stay outside while the daughter went in the executive's office for the interview. The mother was given a magazine to look at. The interview went well. The daughter was honest to say that she had left her previous boring job of eighteen months without giving any notice. That didn't bother the executive. He asked her about how she would get the fourteen miles to work. Realizing her mother wouldn't want her to drive alone, she admitted that she didn't know. Asked if she had a car, she said her dad did but she didn't have a driver's license. That brought about a grin. The executive said he knew someone at the Driver's License Bureau and he made a phone call for his newly-hired secretary to see about a license. She took a written test and had to drive the car. She hadn't seen a road rules book so she made good logic and guesses on the questions. One she missed, "for what was the driver license fee used." How was she to know that? She drove the 1932 Chevy for the test and passed and now had her license to drive to work and start her new job.

She hadn't been back to her boring job to pick up her paycheck. With a sigh of relief she boldly went to the front glass office. She opened the door to talk to one of the managers. She was greeted with sarcasm and given her check with a retort, "And don't use us for a recommendation!" She replied, "Oh, I have a job. Did they call you?"

Morals learned were not to go to job interviews with your mother and dressed alike, don't leave a job except in good standing, and don't drive a car without a license because sometime she may not be so lucky.

CARS AND DRIVING AND TRIPS

The farm girl who learned to drive when she was little soon became a big city driver and drove right through town, She got on US 40 about four miles south from the farm and drove eight miles west as US 40 became Wabash Avenue. At 7th Street which was also US 41 she went south to her job. Where US 40 and US 41 crossed was officially geographically calculated as the Cross Roads of America. Driving her dad's 1932 Chevy to work one morning in about 1950 as she pulled to the left to avoid a bad railroad track bump, there was a funny sound. The car veered off the road to the right. She looked up and the car wheel was going up the road about fifty feet ahead of the car. The car stopped on its own just five feet from a concrete porch of a house. She had to wade through tall wet horseweeds to get the wheel. She put the wheel against the bumper and sat in the car in near tears when her dad's neighbor was going by in his big coal truck. He stopped and took her on to work and said he would tell her dad. Her dad got the wheel back on and picked her up from work and they drove north on US 41 to US 40 and then east to the road to the farm where the wheel had come off the car.

This was the same car that did another funny thing back in 1944. She had driven it down the pavement to her classmates' house Thelma and Alma Cottom. Everything was just fine and she turned off the pavement into their yard. When she got out she noticed instead of both front wheels being straight ahead, they were turned in like cross-eyed. Tears welled up in her eyes and she'd be cryin yet if the History teacher hadn't lived across the road. He came over and saw that the tie rods had come loose. He turned the wheels like they should be and used baling wire to fix the situation.

Her dad still had the two 1930s Chevys in the early 50s, when he bought a 1937 Plymouth that had been stored in a barn and looked brand new. It had some rusted parts underneath that a blacksmith cousin soon fixed. It was steel gray. The right front door opened to the right and the driver front door opened to the left... The right back door opened to the left and the left back door opened to the right. The door latches faced each other in the middle of the car. The car had a heater that must have operated from the battery because it was hot instantly. That car went on lots of trips.

Her dad had a cousin, George Christopher, that was also raised in Burnett Indiana. His aunt Rose took in enough washings to send his cousin to Rose Poly Tech. He became successful as president of Packard Motor Company. The cousin and his wife visited the farm girl's dad and mom pretty often. One time her mom apologized and said she didn't have any refreshments to offer them. She said she had just made a cake and it was a failure because it fell. This cousin said in his deep voice, "By Gawd if you have a cake that fell, give me a piece. I bet it won't be so dry that it will clog your throat." Soon the coffeepot was on and the yellow, soggy, lopsided cake was enjoyed around the round oak table in the dining room. The retired president and his wife had no children and they lived in Tipp City, Ohio. The 1937 Plymouth made a trip to Ohio just fine and looked good in their driveway parked next to a new something, probably a Packard or Studebaker in 1952. It was hilly terrain and you could stand on the back lawn and look across hills to see three or four houses. One was for the family that managed their hog farm, another the cattle, maybe chickens and there was a house down the hill by the road where their bookkeeper lived. The house was a ranch style that might have been ninety feet long. Whether that included the garage is not remembered. It was the first time any of the people from the farm near Fontanet had seen a television. It was a cabinet style with the big fourteen-inch screen. The picture was snowy but the sound was good. The dad's little granddaughter was ready for bed in her ruffled pink nightgown and she was holding on to the television and swaying with the music. The retired president of Packard Motors said in his deep voice, "By Gawd I've seen a lot of fan dancers in my day, but that is the cutest little dancer I have ever seen!" These two cousins that had grown up together had traits instilled in them they never forgot. One turned out to be a coal miner and farmer and the other a college educated executive. Both were cousins that grew up barefoot together with the same values and liked soggy cakes.

The first new car in the family was a 1953 automatic blue Ford. The farm girl had a good job at Commercial Solvents and pondered a long time to see if the new car was a wise decision. Her mother asked, "What took you so long to make up your mind to go from that old 1940 two-door to this nice new car?" She wanted to share the new car with her dad. She'd deliberately leave the keys in it and park it behind his 1937 Plymouth. Most of the time he would ask her to move it until a week before a trip was planned to Houston Texas. He thought he might want to help drive on the trip. He took the new Ford for a drive to get used to it. Didn't take him long to decide he liked that automatic shift.

DID ANCESTORS COME ON MAYFLOWER? YES!

One of her Dad's many favorite cousins lived In Hallettsville Texas and he looked forward to getting out of Indiana. So far he had been to Illinois and Ohio. This was the cousin who was an artist and she had made a pencil drawing of herself while looking in a mirror and sent it to him like a postcard in the mail. The pencil "painting" showed great talent and she entitled it, "Thinking of You." Reminiscing their growing up in Burnett Indiana was like hearing an old movie. They talked about how they had always been told that their family ancestors came to America on the Mayflower. But they knew at that late date, no one could prove it. The farm girl's dad treasured an English Meakin Tea Leaf design ironstone coffee cooler that he said came on the Mayflower. Instead of being a saucer it was about the same size but without the indention to hold a cup. It had a ¾ inch upturned rim. It was made to pour coffee in to cool and to drink out of. After these cousins had both died, several years later the daughter met someone with the same Doty last name. Making conversation she mentioned that she would like to know if they really did come on the Mayflower. This person said he had proof that his family did and knew about a big hard cover book The Doty/Doten Family in America that was written in 1889 with complete family lineage from 1620 to 1887. There was a second printing of this book and she managed to get a copy. To her amazement it included a Noah Doty who died November 18, 1862 and was buried in Otter Creek Township Vigo County Indiana which was in Burnett Indiana. And she knew that this was her dad's grandfather. How unique that the circle had closed and sure enough her dad and his cousin were direct 8th generation descendents of one Edward Doty who came on the Mayflower in 1620. The handed-down coffee cooler did come from England and will be treasured forever with the story that the "Doty's" did come on the Mayflower!

Doty Lineage from Edward Doty who came as an indentured servant to help a family along the voyage to America on the Mayflower. 1st generation Edward, 2nd Samuel, 3rd Joseph, 4th John, 5th Zina, 6th Noah, 7th Zina, 8th Grover and 9th Norma Mae Doty.

Mayflower passengers were ones who left their native country to pursue freedom to worship how they believed. Pilgrims sacrificed comforts to fulfill their convictions for themselves and for the generations to come. Those who know they are descendents of these Pilgrims know they have the genes of the hardy ones who survived the first dreadfully cold winter Those today know their roots were founded with the Pilgrims whose belief in God was foremost in their very being.

The Fontanet farm girl's dad talked a lot about his mother whose name was Dove Creal before marrying Zina Doty. She died at age 50 or so and left memories he cherished. He was proud his mother had bright rich red hair. He remembered she revealed a vivid dream and she described how Heaven was beautiful and angels were coming for her.

Through the years long after her dad passed away, bits and pieces of research and casually acquired stories add to the lore and need to be added for the generations now and to come. One would wonder how Zine and Dovie would have found time to live on a farm and also run a grocery store where she ran the post office while caring for a large family. This was in the Rosedale Indiana rural area.

Dove's father was James Lewis Creal and her mother was Sarah Roselinda Burnett Creal. Children William Lewis and twins, Nancy and Sara died as children. Dove was the only surviving child when her mother died. She was born 1857 and died 1911. Dove's father married Amanda Havens August 23 1885, and fourteen children were born. Living beyond childhood were Rose May born April 16, 1868 and died October 3, 1947: Ida Belle born December 31, 1869 and died in 1934; Charles Clifford born October 8, 1871 and died 1935; Bessie Gertrude born July 21, 1875 and died February 21, 1961; James Burton born March 23, 1877 and died December 11, 1939; Ethel Abby born June 16, 1881 and died July 5, 1934; Ova Beatrice born December 16, 1886 and died 1967. Twins Carrie Agnes born April 19, 1883 and died January 30, 1909 and Katie died April 3, 1886. These were the aunts and uncles that the farm girl's father idolized and talked about a lot. They were half aunts and uncles but loved a whole lot. And the Doty/Creal cousins grew up mostly in the Burnett or Rosedale areas. The Creal's were of Scotch and Welsh descent. The Doty's would have been English having come on the Mayflower. Taken from History of Vigo County 1891 tells that James Lewis Creal was in the carpenter trade until 1858 when he commenced farming except for when he was in the service of his country. He enlisted in 1861 for 3 months and then re-enlisted July 18, 1862 after the death of his first wife, Roselinda (February 1862) til the close of the Civil War. While in the dangerous position as color sergeant, he was wounded in his right hand while carrying the flag and story has it that he switched hands and kept on. He lost his right eye. He was detailed as being a nurse in Knoxville Tennessee and an ambulance driver. He was a prisoner in Libby and Andersonville.

His first wife, Roselinda, and possibly his two-year old twin daughters were killed by wolves and records found in the Terre Haute Library indicate they were buried in the same grave in Burnett Cemetery.

James Lewis Creal was only son of Lewis Vernon Creal and Nancy Messer Creal. Nancy was a midwife and had gone to deliver a baby and was murdered, presumed by Indians, upon her return and was found in the barn.

Father of Lewis Vernon was Anthony married to Hannah Seymour and sketchy correlations are trying to be verified that Jane Seymour, the 2nd wife in the story of Henry VIII might be related... Just when one thinks no other information will be found, an email comes from an inquiry on the name of Creal on the internet that there was the name Seymour who was a brother of Jane. So she may be a many greats aunt. Remains to be proven but anyway if you have Creal in a family tree, you might want to say it is possible that you descended from royalty kinda! And another tidbit. The farm girl remembers her dad talking about an Aunt Rye. She may have been wife of Henry Seymour Creal, Hannah Gray. Her middle name may have been Mariah, but was known as "Rye".

Genealogy and history are intertwined with intrigue and there are always facts that pop up when you might least expect it. The rule of thumb is to have as many records of names, places and dates on hand. Charts with this information let one know what facts are known and the source. Whether it is hearsay, speculation or from a story of someone who remembers what they saw or heard, the stories unwind. James Lewis Creal born 1833 died 1893, son of Lewis Vernon Creal, was the grandson of Anthony Creal and Hannah Seymour. Speculation of fellow Creal researchers is that Anthony's father was

William Creal who was residing in Washington County during 1778 and pledged an Oath of Allegiance, Fidelity and Support to the United States or that Anthony's father was Emmanuel Creal who is recorded on the 1790 Federal census of Bedford, Westchester Co, New York. His mother's maiden name was more than likely Burton or possibly Curtis or Lewis. Thus the fascination to continue researching. Perhaps someone who reads this book will have a fact to add. It is interesting to see the name Lewis and Burton in the names of children.

About 1812 Anthony and his wife Hannah migrated with their children west to Chautauqua County, NY. During 1820 and 1821 two of Anthony's sons and one of his daughters left Chatauqua County with members of the Burnett, Hall and Markle familes and traveled Lake Ontario, Lake Erie and the Erie Canal for their destination Vigo County Indiana. After establishing roots in the adjacent township Otter Creek, the Creals made livings as curriers, farmers and millers. The family grew and spread out near the neighborhoods of Grant Station and Burnett. Here is the name Burnett and there was a Markle mill for many many years that the Fontanet farm girl remembers.

The farm girl's father, Grover Lewis Doty, was born in 1890 wouldn't have remembered his grandfather, James Lewis Creal, who died in 1893. Perhaps his mother did talk about her father but he didn't pass any stories onto his farm girl daughter.

Children (and their spouses) of Zina and Dove M Creal Doty: Edna Agnes married Roscoe Haase, Lena Adalie married Claude Hane, Virgie Gladys married Max Sexton, Delphia married George Lake, Wallace married Mindy Marquis, Clay married Alma Marquis (brothers married sisters), and the farm girl's father, Grover Lewis Doty married Alice Cox.

The farm girl spent many hours with her cousins and combined her love with poems she enjoyed writing.

Sixty Years in This Wicked World for Nuthin

Date: September 12, 1999
To: Max and Maxine Doty Fulmer
By: Norma Mae Doty Taylor

As you both celebrate at the Harvest House today,
I whole-heartedly add my special Happy Birthdays!
I looked and looked and looked, it was so hard
And I never found the Perfect Cards.

I hope my rhyming words express how I feel,
Reminisce as yarns from an old spinning wheel.
Years can't be eighty; it's surely a mistake
But the candles will fit on a Big birthday cake!

No telephones to phone, we just dropped in to meet
To laugh or share a scrumptious meal or special treat!
How I loved Aunt Alma's homemade ice cream
And I thought having a refrigerator was really neat.

After dad died, I thought Uncle Clay was my hero
I'd see him in a crowd and he looked to say hello
He would point his finger, cock his head and wink
His smile melted my heart, tears back I would blink!

Our wonderful parents are remembered with love
As they enjoy their lives ever after in Heaven above!
Kenneth, Margaret and Maxine, Cousins of mine
Raised with my brother, Howard, our many talents shine.

And, Max, we were blessed when you entered the fold
Added so much, many times I hope you have been told!
Four beautiful daughters put on the rosters of family
So, Max and Maxine, enjoy your birthdays Happily!

Norma Mae Doty Taylor

Max and Maxine: (a few days later)

The Celebration is not forgotten, but come and gone
I saw all the cards and packages for Birthdays you won!
How great to almost bust the walls at the Harvest House
I don't think there was room left.. for even a tiny mouse.

I still feel honored to have been included, along with Linda
To see you, your children, grand and great, too many to count on fingers.
I really put a lot of thought about this gala high- societal affair
Planned my dress, jewelry, makeup, and curled my hair.

I took an hour or more to find the earrings right
Not the dangling rhinestones, they're for night
Maybe the bright red ones, No they're too thick,
The three-strand silver ones, they'll do the trick!

Harvest House Parking Lot was jammed full with cars
I was nervous as I wondered how I would fit in so far
I really thought I had done my best, was dressed to the hilt
Felt smug in my sling-back high heeled pumps, felt no guilt.

Yeah, I will fit just fine with these high-fashion cousins
So I stopped worrying, walked right in, and quit my fussin.
I carried my weight well, and enjoyed every moment.
As I left, reached for my ears... my heart sank in sad lament!

Instead of looking my best, I must have looked rather plain
Walking around, piously, head aloof feeling no pain
And no wonder no one gazed or gaped in awe
I must have looked just like any other grandma.

So I blew my chance to make the big impression
And far from being a smashing sensation!
Why don't you have another Birthday celebration, a repeat
And next time I won't leave the earrings laying on the car seat!

Ode to Margaret Doty Stowe
By Norma Mae Doty Taylor

Another Holiday Season and time to reflect
A year of events to ponder and recollect
Some happiness and some sweet sorrow
Always with hope of a bright tomorrow.

Celebrating Thanksgiving and hear the story
Of the First Celebration in 1621 of Pilgrims weary,
They were thankful for survival and Indian friends
Who helped them plant corn to meet their material ends.

We Doty Cousins are thankful for the Mayflower
That brought Edward Doty safely across the bower.
He married Faith Clark and children raised
Our ancestors with stories to amaze.

Half of the ship's passengers did not survive.
The ones who did, were hardy to have stayed alive
Their longing to Worship in Their Beliefs
Gave them strength to share joy and their griefs.

PS:

Margaret: I saw your strength, your passion
Mourning Maxine in a stately fashion
I thank God for being a Doty and knowing you
Your talent, your caring traits to name a few.

You and I are alike, in that we're the last
Of the Clay and Grover Doty's of recent past.
Our brothers Kenneth and Howard passed away so sad
And then Maxine..... Will you now be my sister I never had!

Norma Mae Doty Taylor

Celebrating the 90th Young birthday for Margaret on November 16, 2003 was awesome. The hall on Lafayette Avenue in Terre Haute was jam packed with ones from 9 weeks to 90! Five generations. Family resemblances were evident. Food galore and laughter abounded. A video prepared as a gift was professional, personal, sad and funny. The musical background was beautiful and appropriate! Pictures were shown of the farm girl's Uncle Clay and Aunt Alma, who were parents of Margaret. The memories flooded over her. She thought too of the Mayflower with about as many passengers as there were people there. She marveled that the pilgrim Edward Doty was one who survived the first terrible cold winter. Because he did, all the ones at this celebration were blessed. Would Edward ever have imagined how just one tiny segment of his offspring would be gathered to celebrate the birthday of a 9th generation granddaughter. And she thought that the traits of all were ones to be proud. Gourmet cooks, all dressed in wonderfully tasteful styles, friendly personalities, fun-loving ones who appreciated one another and their heritage

ODE TO DOTY COUSINS

When I think of something that I know should be told
I ought to set right down and write it before I'm too old.
I'd tell of those I remember or stories I've heard about Doty Cousins.
Aunts and Uncles and we Cousins by the Duzzins.
First cousins: Russell, Delbert, George (Elvis), Lester Hane, Mable Termin,
Inez Burns, Armeda Kendall, also Hane before they changed their name.
The Haase's: Tom, Carson, Bill, Don, Vivian Burkett, Wilma Shelton, Iva
Cress, Martha Marrow.
We share memories of fun together, stories we've heard, and sweet sorrow
And there are more
Etta Doty Smith, Wanda Doty Diehl, Kenneth Doty, Margaret Doty Stowe,
Maxine Doty Fulmer; and Charles (Chink) Lake
Bonnie, Betty and Gerry Sexton
Howard Doty and Norma Mae Doty Taylor.
Some already departed this earthly life and some remain
But all embraced with Angels in rich sweet communion
Rejoicing for the Heavenly Doty Cousin Reunion!

Pages of History, Impressions for Marks are made
With heritages for generations of ancestors so staid.
Their integrity, perseverance, and instilled beliefs are Ours
To cherish and cultivate for our Shining Hours.
Zina Doty and Dovie Creal married and made a home.
Children: Edna, Lena, Virgie, Delphia, Wallace, Grover and Clay
Was their family that made us what we are today!
Happy memories, appreciated Christian traits, and their Love
Laid the stepping stones on the path for Heavenly Homes Above.

We Doty Cousins know from where we come
Have carved our way with records in God's book of what we've done!
We're 9th Generation from Edward Doty
Who courageously sailed the Mayflower on perilous sea, made his way
To land in 1620 at Plymouth Rock in Massachusetts USA.
He married Faith Clarke and started the generations of Doty Cousins
And we're the heirs of their production of all the Doty Cousins by the
Duzzins!

COX, BEARD, SPARKS, ROHRER

The farm girl's mother didn't talk much about where she came from. Many years later bits and pieces came together and would have been good if she had known. Her father's parents, David and Sarah Beard Cox, lived in Staunton Township Virginia and were thought to be quite wealthy. A disagreement over the slave issue embittered her grandfather to leave his father. Story has it that he packed his wife in an oxcart to journey to a new home. They settled in New Goshen Indiana where many children were born, including the farm girl's grandfather, Harvey.

Harvey's grandchildren many years later, pieced hearsay information and figured out how their grandfather who lived in New Goshen met their grandmother, Laura Virginia Sparks, who was born in Niles Township near Chicago. Old letters and land records prove that Laura came from the Chicago area as a young girl with her parents who bought land in St Joseph Twp in Champaign County Illinois. Harvey Cox was working on the railroad that was built and being repaired near where Levi and Helen Sparks lived with their family, including Laura. The farm girl's cousin, Sarah, remember hearing the story that Laura and her sisters were playing and walking along the railroad when some boys followed them and were being "naughty" and pushing the girls. One of the young men working noticed it and he took a stand against the boys and told them to leave the girls alone and was stern enough that the boys left. Laura "set her cap for him" and just knew she was going to get better acquainted. Harvey and Laura married in Champaign County Illinois in 1884 and had one daughter, Flora. The next daughter, Ethel, was born in Scott County Kansas and the third daughter, Edith, was born in Vigo County Indiana.

On the Cox side of the family the farm girl's great great grandfather was Jacob Cox married to Annie Eaves. Father of Jacob was Phillip.

Searching for historical and genealogical lore, Wayne Cox found the Old Providence Cemetery in Virginia where Jacob was buried and inquired of another visitor if anybody knew of these old Cox relatives. Delighted and much surprised, he was directed to a house nearby where the Cox families had lived in the early 1800s. And kinfolk still lived in this old homeplace. It was a most unlikely coincidence and wonderful experience for these relatives to meet and become friends. Any hard feelings that happened to break up the family in the mid 1850s pre Civil War days, were not present and the gap was bridged and more trips were made by Wayne from Indianapolis to Virginia. Wayne's father, Elmer Cox, and the Fontanet farm girl's mother were first cousins. They were great grandchildren of the Jacob buried in Virginia, which made Wayne and the farm girl great great grandchildren.

Sarah Beard was born in March 1833 in Brownsburg, Rockbridge Virginia and married David Cox June 1 1854 in Rockbridge Virginia. Her grandfather was Peter Sr Beard born in the 1750s and died about 1817. He was married to Catherine ? and her father and mother were David Beard, born 1799 in Augusta County Virginia and died 1870/72 in Rockville Parke County Indiana. He married Mary A Shuey May 4 1826 in Augusta Virginia. She was born May 4 1800 in Augusta Virginia and was the daughter of John Ludwig (Lewis) Shuey and Mary Lash.

Cemetery visits can be awesome when descendents stand in plots and read inscriptions on grave stones.

Those who can ponder with closed eyes, imaginations might see horses and buggies assembled with mourners not knowing that a hundred years later, there would be ones who come to pay respect and reflect. The blood of the deceased would flow into veins of generations to come. They wouldn't know that great great great grandchildren, great nieces and nephews and other kin would come from many states in transportation of airplanes, trains and automobiles to visit the graves. Never could they have imagined.

In 1886 the grandparents of the farm girl's mother, Levi Allen and Helen Virginia Rohrer Sparks, sold a tract of land in Champaign County Illinois and they journeyed to Scott County Kansas to homestead. Some old letters reveal that the Sparks' loaded their goods on a train to go as far as possible before the final trek to the available land to homestead. The farm girl's grandparents, Harvey and Laura Cox, went along but only stayed a year or so before coming back to the Midwest in Indiana to be near the father's family in Vigo County.

There was a hardy pioneer-spirited woman, Marietta Crookshanks, who was born in Virginia across the river from Marietta, West Virginia. The Crookshanks family came to the Missouri area in 1866 by covered wagon when Marietta was 3 years. The farm girl's third cousin has a walnut dresser that was brought on that covered wagon to Missouri. Having a treasured heirloom with a story is worth much more than the antique value. The third cousin shared the story of her grandparents. Her grandmother, Marietta (later to be referred to in a letter as Ettie) was a daring pioneer woman. This young woman rode her horse several miles to join a wagon train passing through Missouri. She sold her horse to pay the way and bought as many supplies as she could, including some lumber and nails. She homesteaded in

Scott County Kansas next to land of John Sparks. They fell in love and married and lived in a sod house. They had two or three children before going back to Missouri. John Sparks was brother of the farm girl's grandmother, Laura Virginia. He sometimes visited his sister who lived on a farm in Vigo County Indiana.

Levi and his family stayed the full five years and much history is derived from letters her great grandmother wrote telling of the hardships of having to shovel tunnels in snow to care for livestock in primitive shelters. The homesteaded land was sparse of trees and quick shelter living quarters were dug into hillsides and sod was used as roofs. The great grandmother wrote of counting the days until they had finished the time required to have earned their land. They sold the remote farm they developed before settling in the Wichita Kansas area and posed for a picture sitting in front of the Rug Weaving sign on their house. Three generations later the story was unraveled when three third cousins, Norma, Helen and Nadine, met in Brookfield Missouri. It was awesome as they held the large hardback Bible that their great grandmother, Helen Virginia Rohrer Sparks, had written the names of their grandparents and the dates they were born in the 1800s.

Births: Levi Allen Sparks June 23, 1830 and Helen Virginia Rohrer December 25, 1838. Their children George Allen Sparks January 15, 1858, Ann Elisabeth Sparks September 16, 1859, John Lovell Sparks March 27, 1861, Laura Virginia Sparks February 5, 1863, Agnes Rebecca Sparks February 23, 1865, Ralph Jerome Sparks March 22, 1867, Florence Clyde Sparks June 9, 1869 and Francis Oliver Sparks November 30 1871.

John was grandfather of Helen and Nadine and Laura was grandmother of Norma.

The farm girl has a box full of historical and genealogical information. One such is a copy of the front cover of a program of Scott County Kansas Celebrating 100 years! 1886 – 1986. This was recorded proof that her great grandparents, Levi Sparks and Helen Virginia Rohrer Sparks, were among the hardy pioneer-minded ones who were the first settlers. Champaign County Illinois St Joseph Township Records show that Levi and Helen Sparks sold land July 1, 1886 to John S Brookbank for $3600. And letters support homesteading journey. In a letter dated April 6, 1887 from J. S. Rohrer (from Red Bluff, California, to another brother. As follows: "Dear Brother and Sister, Well as I have a bit of leisure time I will rite you a few lines in answer to yours of 27th of Feb. Well in the first place I am in good health and getting fat again. I lost flesh at first here but have got use to the climate so that I have got it most back again. Yes, I hear from others. The Sparks.s left Urbana (Illinois) the 25th of November. Levi, Ralph and Ollie went with there things he loaded a car and went through with it. Jinny & Clyde (girl Florence Clyde), stayed with Florence (Rohrer) a couple days then went to Jim's a few days then went out to her new home. They got through all right and liked the country. You wanted to know what they got for there old place at that time. I did not know but in Jinnies last she said they sold it to Brookbank for $30 per acre he did not get a very good price considering that he had put in a good bit of tile and had it fairly drained. They are at Terry Finney County Kansas. George and John and Laura and Levi all live in different places so they are scattered. As to Ralph Sparks he is in Kansas and whether he is still wanting to be a carpenter. No I did not know that they had built the new road. They surveyed a rail road by here yesterday. It comes up the creek this far then leavs the creek to cross the hills. There will be a station within 200 yards of my house. Well Jinnie (not the Jinnie for Virginia Rohrer Sparks), you forgot to tell me how you settled the babys name and to tell me what it is so let me know in your next. Well they done pretty well stiring up sinners there and a little of the same kind of work would not hurt these parts. Will rite soon, Your brother J S Rohrer."

Another letter also written depicts how it was as they homesteaded in Kansas. It is copied from the original letter written on browned with age lined tablet paper to son, John, and wife.(The Marietta mentioned above) "March the 20th Terry Kansas Dear Son and family, I will try to answer your letter received a few days ago. We was all glad to hear from you. We are well at present. Father has been ailing he is troubled with diarrhree but is better now and I too had a sick spell but am all right now and hope this will find you all well. I am glad you like your new home. Father wants to follow you. Ever since you left here he has been so dissadisfied and sais he wont stay here very long after our 5 years are out. He wants you to write and tell him if he could do anything with his cattle thar says he will drive them through. He could not do very well farming and would want to raise cattle as that is easier work for him. Of course we would have to grow enough corn to fatten to sell. Ollie is anxious to get home again. I had a letter yesterday. He wants to work at his job till last of june but sais if he is needed he will come in 4 or 5 weeks. Father thinks we better let him stay to earn as much as he can at his job, he sais George Mitchell is poorly and has been for a month and sais he would not be able to hold his place if he did not have Ollie to fire up mornings and help him. Annie (her daughter who lived in Evanston near Chicago) sent us a box of goods I got 3 sateen and one calico dresses. Clyde (Florence Clyde) a sateen a scotch ziphir a gingham and an embroidery white dress. We are ever so well pleased with the things. There is a corset for

Clyde and 4 embroideried handkerchiefs to divide. Dan Battershells little girl died in feb. She had fits from 15 to 25 an hour was totally blind for a month before she died. Dan was here last day of feb and stayed all night. Father found your rope and chain next morning after you left and layed rite by the clothes line post. It was only a few steps from where your wagon set, and your shoe thread was left here. Well now what kind of society is thare I reckon lots of drunken men whare thare is a saloon about every other house. How far are you from Town and what kind of churches are thare. Do you go to meetings any place and are thare any churches close around you and how are the schools and how do things sell thare groceries I mean. Dried apples are 20 cents per lb and green apples are 50 cents a peck here. I tried to get dried ones at Terry yesterday but thare was none. We have 8 fresh cows George one and Ralph one. The cattle all seem to be doing all right only one cow had not got along well her calf is a week old. We lost 7 head 5 died and 2 disapeared. We have heard nothing of them yet, the weather is rough and cold most of the time and had another snow last week. I haven't made any garden yet, we don't make any butter to sell as we let the calves run to the cows. Aunt Annie blames your sister Annie for coaxing Ollie away from her and I think it was your letter to Ollie that made him leave her and go to Frannie June. She was dredfully put out because he did not go back to stay with her after he had been to Chicago, Well I gues I have told you all for this time so write soon. Love to you all from Ma to John and Ettie. Oh yes Ralph is building 2 mills one is for a man east of us he is to get 22$ for it the other is for Mr Taylor 4 miles north he furnishes his own material and Ralph is to build it for 10$."

More history and genealogy is proven with obituaries and newspaper clippings. How fascinating for descendents but also of interest to those who enjoy hearing "how it used to be."

Headlined: "Former Resident of Scott City dead. Levi Sparks, a former resident of this vicinity and father of Mrs U G Ruth (Florence Clyde Sparks Ruth) died at his home in Pontiac Illinois September 17 1916. Mr Sparks and family lived here in the early days, leaving here sixteen years ago. He had been living in Pontiac about nine months. We copy from the following account of the death and burial of Mr. Sparks from the Pontiac Daily News: Levi Sparks died at the home of his son, George Sparks, 701 East John Street this city (Pontiac) Sunday morning, Sept 17, after a long illness, death being due to the infirmities of old age. The funeral was held this afternoon at 2:30 from the residence of his son and wife. Rev M L O'Harra, pastor of the First Methodist Episcopal church, conducting the services. Burial was in southside cemetery. Levi Sparks was born January 22, 1830 in Shelby County Indiana and died in Pontiac Illinois September 17, 1916 at the age of eighty-six years, seven months and twenty-five days. When he was four years old he moved with his parents to Chicago where he grew to manhood and in that city on September 24 1856 he was married to Helen V Rohrer who still survives. For sixty years they were permitted to be companion in life. In 1868 they moved to Champaign Illinois. In 1886 they went to western Kansas. Eight children were born to them one dying in infancy. The seven living are George A, Pontiac; Mrs. Anna Mitchell, Chicago; John L, Browning Mo; Mrs. Laura V Cox, Brazil Indiana; Ralph J, Kirksville Mo; Mrs. Florence Clyde Ruth, Scott City KS, and Francis O, Nevada Mo. There are twenty-four grandchildren and four great grandchildren. Some forty years ago, Mr. Sparks was converted and joined the United Brethren church, remaining in that church until his coming to Pontiac when he came into the Methodist.

Mr. Sparks was a genuine Christian manifesting in his daily life the excelencies of the moral and spiritual virtues. He was of a quiet, unassuming nature, a man of substantial worth. In unostentatious strength of character he lived his life among men, and with the calmness of the Christian heart, and the assurance of the Christian faith, he went to be with God."

Here was the word "converted" in the obituary three generations from the farm girl. Her great grandfather was converted in a United Brethren church. It was also a United Brethren church she joined at age 6 and experienced her conversion while at a United Brethren church camp at age 14. As stories and facts are researched and recorded much is learned about who we are.

Another newspaper obituary in the Pontiac The Daily Leader on Wednesday May 19, 1920: "Remains of Mrs. Levi Sparks Brought Here for Interment. The remains of the late Mrs. Levi Sparks, who died at Evanston, Ill, Tuesday were brought to this city last night and taken to the home of her son, George Sparks, on North John Street. The funeral services will be held at 10 Thursday morning from the First Methodist Episcopal Church with Rev M L O'Harra conducting the service. Burial will be in the south side cemetery. Miss Helen Virginia Rohrer was born at Newtown Virginia December 25, 1838 where she remained until reaching the age of seventeen when she removed to Evanston. She was united in marriage there to Levi Sparks on September 24, 1851. Following her marriage she resided for a time at Wichita Kan and later in Evanston for a number of years. She leaves by her death the following sons and daughters: George of this city, John of Browning Mo, Ralph of Chillicothe Mo, Francis O of Nevada Mo, Mrs. Anna Mitchell of Chicago, Florence Clyde of Scott City Kan and Mrs. Laura Cox of Brazil Ind."

Another cog in the wheel of the lives of Levi and Helen Rohrer Sparks. In a Wichita Directory dated 1909 there is listed a Levi A (Helen V). as carpet weaver 1511 Ida Ave so that is where they settled after leaving the bleak homesteaded farm in Scott County Kansas and maybe there until they went to Pontiac Illinois.

A generation on back would be the following for the parents of her great grandfather Levi Allen Sparks. Another treasured morsel of genealogy information, the farm girl shares is a copy from a document written in beautiful script ink: "L Sparks & E Conley application for marriage license. "Be it remembered that on the twenty sixth day of January one thousand eight hundred and twenty seven, the following Marriage License was issued by me Hiram Aldridge Clerk of Shelby Circuit Court State of Indiana, Shelby County for the State of Indiana, to any person legally authorized to Solemnize the rights of Matrimony greeting know ye that License is hereby granted to Levi Sparks and Elizabeth Conley to be joined together as husband and wife in the honorable bounty of Matrimony accordingly as the Seal of our Said County hereunto affirmed at Shelbyville."

Another copy from the ledger also recorded in the same handwriting: Certificate of Marriage was filed: "I, Adam Wright, the Justice of the peace for Shelby County, do hereby certify that on the 1st day of February Eighteen Hundred Twenty Seven Levy Sparks and Elizabeth Conley were married together as husband and wife by me. Adam Wright."

Thus Levi Sparks and Elizabeth Conley Sparks were parents of Levi Allen Sparks.

Parents of Helen Virginia Rohrer were John Henson Rohrer born January 10 1813 in Washington County Maryland married March 24 1836 to Rebecca Samsell born July 21, 1816 and died November 21 1864 and buried in Niles Township Cook County Illinois. Their children were mostly born in Virginia. Newtown, Frederick County was the homeplace of her father, Johan Samsel. John was buried in Mayview Cemetery on Illinois Route 136 near St Joseph in Champaign County Illinois. His great great granddaughter (the farm girl), his great great great grandson, Tracy Taylor and his daughters visited his grave. Three generations had their pictures taken beside the tall thin marble grave stone of John Henson Rohrer. Tracy was quick to notice the wisdom that the cemetery plot was maybe the first one chosen and it was on the highest point of the otherwise flat terrain of the country. The little girls were in awe that this was their ancestor who was born in 1813. Tasheena (later being known as Sheena) and Bridget Taylor will remember this day and it will help them know their heritage. Another of three sisters, Hollie Niccole Taylor, wasn't there that day so she will need to visit this cemetery along with her sisters again as a tradition to pass along to those who will become great great great and great and know that these ancestral physical traits are the genes and the blood that is in their veins.

The grave was visited by the 6th generation and the farm girl (now grandmother) has a copy of the will of John Hensen Rohrer that was written in St Joseph Township May 11, 1871 and filed for probate July 5, 1871 by J W Shuck, County Clerk of Champaign County. Some quotes are: "My son, Samuel and my daughters Frances and Florence shall remain upon the farm and occupy the house until the first day of March 1872 and with the guidance of the executors by me appointed hereafter mentioned shall cultivate and harvest the crops now growing and shall have such portion of the proceeds of the farm and use of personal property as their circumstances shall require. And I further declare that the farm shall be rented to great and competent persons until my children Samuel and Florence shall become of age.

To my eldest son John I give and bequeath one dollar. To my daughters Anna Rebecca I bequeath one hundred dollars which shall be paid to her before any general division of my property so made. To my daughter Frances Lavenia I give one hundred dollars to be paid to her also before any general division is made. Also further give and bequeath to my daughter Frances the bed upon which she has been herafore sleeping. To my son Samuel I give his bed which he occupies and also the three year old gray horse colt. Each to have possession of the above mentioned articles of personal property on the first day of March AD 1872. To my son Melville Lincoln I give one hundred dollars to be paid to him as collected from the sale of real estate. The residue of my personal property I desire to be sold on or about the first day of March AD 1872. The money raised from the sale shall be applied towards the payment of any debts which may be owed by me. I hereby give and bequeath all the remainder of my property, goods and chattels to my daughters Helen Virginia, Anna Rebecca, Mary Elizabeth, Laura Catherine, Frances Lavenia, Florence Edmonsen, and to my son Samuel who shall share and share equally on such division. In addition I give to my son Samuel one third of the corn now planted and growing upon the farm. The corn to be gathered by him and two thirds placed in the crib. And to my daughter Florence Edmonia in addition to what I have already bequeathed to her I give my bed upon which I have heretofore slept and on which now lie for her own use and benefit."

One would ponder the simplicity or enormity of the worth of this John Hensen Rohrer. His daughter Helen Virginia as mentioned in the will was the farm girl's great grandmother. The one who married Levi Sparks.

It is treasured experience to visit old cemeteries and know you are standing on hallowed ground where earthly remains are buried. If you are quiet you can imagine the mourners in the fashion of the day in horse and buggy. Little would they know that for decades to come, kinfolk would come to visit the graves. Located not far from Shirkieville near New Goshen Indiana where David and Sarah Cox settled is the Rosehill Cemetery. David died April 27 1900, his wife Sarah died March 27 1877 in childbirth with baby in same grave. They had fourteen other children and some died early and are buried there also. Ones living to adults were James H, John L, Dosier, Harvey (the farm girl's grandfather), Franklin, twins David Ira and Sarah Ida, and Walter. Ida married Frank Lemons so there are lots of Cox's and Lemons' who are related

The Cox', Beard's, Sparks' and Rohrer's had a story and they didn't live sixty years in this world for nuthin.

COUSIN ODDS AND ENDS

The farm girl's Cox cousins could write a book with all they have done. The farm girl lived just up the road apiece from her Uncle David and Aunt Leona. Her cousin Betty took lessons and played the piano. The farm girl loved to hear her play the spirited march, "Under the Double Eagle." Betty and Elsie were hard workers and often helped their dad when he baled hay for farmers. Betty laughed one time and said they were her dad's "boys" but said it sure was fun to go to town on Saturdays to spend the money they earned for girl stuff. Rosemary was the youngest and the farm girl played often with her. These cousins walked many times to Fontanet to the United Brethren church or to doings at school about a mile and half away. Rosemary married Floyd Burriss, her childhood sweetheart. At a Cox cousin reunion many years later, the farm girl "smart alecky" unpacked her dinner basket and proudly announced that the chocolate cake was made from scratch. Elsie, her equally smart alecky clever cousin. said, "From scratch? That is what we feed our chickens." Of course, what she meant was the cake was made from a recipe and not a cake from a "box" that had just become popular in the grocery stores.

Her Cox cousin, Betty, married Dave Salmoni, who was an electrician. The farm girl and her mother and Aunt Leona visited them in Michigan, Flat Rock maybe, but it was close to Detroit. Betty couldn't get the country out of her, and she and Dave had a sizeable chicken operation and sold broilers and eggs almost "in town." On this same trip they visited a Doty cousin, Mable Hane Termin, who lived in Ohio, maybe Toledo. They raised horses and her husband competed in harness races. The farm people thought his sulky and bright colored satin attire was impressive. The farm girl drove her 1953 blue Ford and did not like driving through the tunnel under all that water of the Hudson River to Windsor Canada. These country folks went to Niagara Falls and marveled at its splendor and beauty. Her Aunt Leona was perturbed that while going through customs, both coming and going, her's was the only suitcase that was opened and pawed through leaving everything in disarray.

Hazel and Raymond spent a lot of time with their grandparents. Raymond joined the Marines soon after he graduated from Fontanet and often talked about being at Pearl Harbor. Hazel has a memory of an elephant, a sweet elephant, and loves to talk about how it was at Grandma and Grandpa Cox'es. She remembers when her grandma's brother, John, came from Missouri once to visit. He brought a RADIO with him and how excited everyone was to get to put on the headphones and HEAR music and voices. Each one only had a short turn because their great Uncle John said, "The battery would soon run down."

One time when the Christiansen cousins visited their grandparents, the youngest Eugene was maybe 5 or 6. His mother, Edith Cox Christiansen, drove from Billings Montana when the farm girl still lived on the farm. Her dad loved showing the city kids things on the farm. There were hickory nuts on the ground and Gene was so excited that the nuts had their coats on. His Uncle Grover probably told him they had hulls on... Within the next sixty years the farm girl went to Seattle to visit her cousins Betty and Arnold (who called himself Chris). Betty drove her cousin all around the city with its steep hills and she and husband, Alan, drove further east in the state to the foot of the mountains and enjoyed scrumptious chocolates from a Swiss shop. Betty said her family always lived in Montana far away from the roots in Indiana and thought they had missed a lot of the family traditions. She was glad to hear stories and did remember visiting a few times. Chris was retired and he took his cousin all over in Snohomish, Maryville and Everett and to Taylor's Landing in Mukilteo. She had her picture taken in front of Taylors Landing and wrote home that she had bought the place. The sea food there was so good. It was fun watching the ferry boats load with many cars and big trucks.

The farm girl when she was grown, traveled west on the train and journeyed the northern Amtrak route from Mattoon, Chicago, Minneapolis, northern Montana, through Idaho to Everett Washington. She remembers how the evergreens on the east side of the mountains were snow covered. Reaching the top and going down the west side of the mountains it was like spring with less snow and then the flowering trees. Fields of yellow daffodils and tulips as far as could be seen. It was March 7 and still very much winter back in the Midwest. She intended to stay a week but stayed until the last few days of her limited extension time of thirty days. Cousins, all so much alike who appreciated being together, like peas in a pod.

Norma Mae Doty Taylor

ODE TO COX COUSINS

When I think of something that I know should be told
I ought to set right down and write it before I'm too old
I'd tell about reunions we've had with Cox Cousins,
Aunts and Uncles and we Cousins by the Duzzin.
We remember Lewis, Ronald and Phillip Montague
Hurley and Charles Green, and Aaron Lauher too
Arnold Christiansen, Raymond Hollingsworth,
Howard Doty and Elsie Cox Perry
All embraced with Angels in rich sweet communion
Rejoicing for the Heavenly Cox Cousin Reunion!

When Harvey Cox married Laura Virginia Sparks in 1884
They established a bond with a home that spun tales of lore.
Happy memories, appreciated Christian traits, and their Love
Laid the stepping stone on the path for Heavenly Homes Above.
Love abounds with we earthling Cox Cousins:
Hazel Hollingsworth Webster, Imogene Green Fox,
Betty Christiansen Meyers and Gene Christiansen,
Rose Mary Cox Burriss and Betty Cox Salmoni
Sarah Bell Montague Conard and ME – Norma Mae Doty Taylor.

GENEALOGY IN A NUTSHELL FROM HERE AND THERE

Ever ending searches and accumulations of names, dates, stories unfold information where it is least expected. Diligent seeking and sharing is amazing when it is studied. To realize the importance of sources of records that were hand written hundreds of years ago, for research into for county and state archives, for computers and the internet is nearly overwhelming when one can see a chart for generations back. Preserving names and stories and dates is something everyone should do for their family and for the generations to follow. As thoughts come, make notes for all to know from whence they come, for how they were taught and why. It will even acquaint one more to their self.

Having red hair was not as common as dark or light. The farm girl's father talked often of his mother's red hair. She may have gotten it from the Creal side of her family. He had a little sister he adored and talked of her long red curls and was saddened when he talked of her death when she was four years old. Her name was Captolia and he called her Cappy. The farm girl has a cousin, Bonnie, who remembers her mother, Virgie, talking about a little sister, Cappy, but there isn't any mention of her in cemetery records. She would probably have been in Burnett and maybe in the part of the cemetery that was disrupted when the railroad went through. She remembers reading in something when she was a little girl about Cappy and also vaguely about twin babies who didn't live. She thinks it may have been an old Bible and regrets no one knows what would have happened to it. The farm girl's second cousins came to visit and her dad always admired Margie with her red hair. The farm girl had a woven doll buggy and has pictures of Margie's little sister, Judy, sitting in it with her very blonde hair.

Norma Mae Doty Taylor

Two dark haired sisters, one called Sissy (her name was Viola Maxine named for her two aunts) and then along came Nancy. They lived in Burnett. Often the farm girl and her parents would stop by on their way back to Fontanet from Terre Haute. It pleased their great Uncle Grover when they wanted to go home with him and their Aunt Alice. And the farm girl too. All these little girls grew up to be ambitious and talented. They owned and operated elegant restaurants, had craft exhibits and sales boutiques in Bridgeton Indiana, especially during the annual infamous Park County Covered Bridge Festivals. Their weddings were awesome with their own designs. The farm girl still marvels at the beautiful gowns and decorations of one wedding at the Burnett Church. She remembers three other second cousins, Mary Jo, Linda and Darla Doty, daughters of her first cousin Kenneth and his wife Inez. The wedding was probably Mary Jo's and it could have been a Gone With the Wind at Tara. These Doty cousins sing and sew, paint and create, cook and bake and the farm girl wonders if she was behind the door when all these talents were passed out.

There is established verified lineage that makes Doty descendent daughters eligible for the D.A.R. (Daughters of Revolution). Abraham VanSickle was a Minuteman in 1774, a member of a group of armed men pledged to take the field at a minute's notice during and immediately before the American Revolution. Abraham VanSickle's daughter Sarah married Joseph Perry Gray, had daughter Sarah Jane Gray who married Noah Doty, who had son Zina Doty, who had son Grover Lewis Doty, who had daughter Norma Mae Doty whose daughter and granddaughters and greats are eligible. Any other females who have the same lineage are those also proven eligible. For the records Abraham VanSickle married Mary Jewell...

The grandmother maiden names are equally as significant for genealogy and family history. Anyone who finds a name that matches their own might very well be "kissin cuzzins."

DOTY: Edward Doty married Faith Clark in Plymouth Massachusetts sixth of January 1634/35, Samuel to Jane Harmon 15 November 1678, Joseph to Sarah Badgly, John born circa 1725 married first to Sarah Potter who died 1759 and then married Sarah Clark (who was the mother of Zina), Zina born 1783 in New Providence Jew Jersey and died March 1834 in Butler County Ohio married Sarah Moore where their remains are in the graveyard one mile north of Princeton Butler County, Noah born 3 July 1826 in Hamilton Ohio and died 13 Nov 1867 in Otter Creek Township Indiana married Sarah Jane Gray in 1852 and Sarah died in 1926 in Indianapolis Indiana, Zina born 18 March 1855 in Ohio and died 3 January 1919 in Burnett Indiana married Dove Creal who was daughter of James and Linda Creal, Grover Lewis born 14 September 1890 married Alice Lillian Cox.

BURNETT: Norma Mae Doty – Grover Lewis Doty b 1890 – Dove Creal (married Zina Doty) – Roselinda (Rosalinda) Burnett b 1801 Caldwell NJ (married James Lewis Creal) – Justus Burnett b 1760 Bottle Hill NJ (married Lois Crane) The farm girl has copies of original drawing of a business which would have been on the main street of Terre Haute, Wabash Avenue. It was Burnett Hides and Tannery. And she has a copy of a drawing of a Creal farm with a big house and barn and livestock that was near Burnett, Indiana.. Both are impressive and showed ambition, integrity and success.

CREAL: Norma Mae Doty – Grover Lewis Doty – Dove Creal – James Lewis Creal – Lewis Vernon Creal b 1809

– Anthony Creal b 1770 (m Hannah Seymour)– William Creal (m ? Burton) Note: Probably was Burton because first child of Anthony and Hannah Creal was Burton Creal.

Census information copied from Vigo County 1850 Otter Creek Township: William Burnett 62 years male Blacksmith, born in New Jersey. Wife Sarah age 42, born New York: Children Malinda 16 years, Emma I age 11, George 9 years, Isabel age 3 all born in New York. Anthony Creal 49 years occupation Miller born in New York, Wife Melinda age 43 born in Indiana. Children Henry age 19, Hildah age 17, Mark A age 9 and John age 2 all born in Indiana. Looked like Lonis (but must be Lewis) age 40 occupation farmer born in New York, Wife Nancy age 39 born in Virginia with one son James L age 17 born in Indiana. A conclusion would be that Malinda Burnett is the one who married James L Creal and were the great grandparents of the girl who played the part of the old woman in the junior class play at Fontanet in 1945

SEYMOUR: Hannah Seymour b 1770 New Cannan Ct, Ezra Seymour b 1748 – Thomas Seymour b 1632 (m Hannah Marvin) - Matthew Seymour b 1669 (m Sarah Hayes – Richard Seamer b 1604 – Robert Seamer. Recently a clue might have been found from a Christine Creal (maiden name).. who is interested in establishing identity with the Creal side of her family. She remembers seeing a chart back to a Seymour who was the brother of Jane Seymour, a wife of Henry VIII. She bore a son and then she died. That may be the link that connects with Creal's passing down the story there was a connection with Jane Seymour, the queen.

COX: Norma Mae Doty – Alice Lillian Cox (m Grover Doty) - Harvey Cox - David Cox (m Sarah Beard) – Jacob Cox (m Anna Eaves – Phillip Cox

The David and Sarah Beard Cox Family: Dosier married Laura Stultz with children: Sylvia, Elmer, Arthur and William; Frank married Ella with children Everett, Iva, Herman, Floyd and Chester; Jim and not sure who married. Maybe another Laura (no children); Walter married Frieda with children: Forest, Elmer, Jenny, Paul, Raymond and Carl; John married Mindy Compton with children Gertie and Grace; Ira (twin to Ida) married Dora Lambert with one daughter Letha; Ida married Frank Lemons with children Emerson, Orpha, Virgil, Gladys, Russell, Dallas and Erline; Harvey married Laura Sparks with children: Flora, Ethel, Edith, Alice, Rosie, Eva, David and Herbert

BEARD: Norma Mae Doty – Alice Lillian Cox, Harvey Cox, David Cox (m. Sarah Beard). Bits of info – Rockbridge County Virginia census in 1850. David Beard is 51 a farmer born in Virginia. Mary is 51 born in Virginia and their children were listed as Samuel 19, <u>Sarah J</u> 17, Jacob 15, Susan 13, David S, 11 and Otterbein G 8 years all born in Virginia.

In 1860 they are not in Virginia, Vigo County Indiana or Park County Indiana. David and Sarah Cox are listed in Vigo County census.

In 1870, William, Jacob, and Susan are in Parke County and David, the father, is living with Jacob. Mary A Shuey Beard is buried at the Teague Cemetery north of Rockville Indiana. She was born August 15 1800 and died September 15 1862.

In 1870 William is listed as 42 and he was already married to wife Mary same age. The farm girl muses that probably her great grandmother Cox, was the daughter of David Beard and married David Cox.

In 1880 William is in Kansas with David S. Jacob is still in Parke County...

SPARKS: Norma Mae Doty – Alice Lillian Cox – Levi Sparks (m Helen V Rohrer) – Levi Sparks (Elizabeth Conley)

ROHRER: Norma Mae Doty – Alice Lillian Cox – Laura Virginia Sparks (m Harvey Cox) - Helen Virginia Rohrer (m Levi Allen Sparks) – John Henson Rohrer (m Rebecca Samsell)

Much history is gained from obituary clippings such as:

Herbert Otis Cox – 17 years old, died at 2 o'clock yesterday morning at the home of his parents, Mr. and Mrs. Harvey W Cox, one mile southeast of Fontanet, after an extended illness. He is survived by six sisters, Mrs Florence Montague Cairo Michigan, Mrs. John Lauher, Oakland Ill, Mrs. Edith Christiansen, Mrs. Alice Doty and Mrs. Eva James of Terre Haute, Mrs. Rosa Hollingsworth of Fontanet and one brother David Cox of Rural Brazil. The funeral will be held at the Mount Aetna church at 11 o'clock Sunday morning and burial will be in the Burnett cemetery.

Mrs. Laura Virginia Cox - 76 years old died at the residence near Fontanet. Surviving are one son, David of rural Brazil, six daughters, Mrs. Flora Montague of Cayuga Indiana, Mrs. Ethel Scharf of Gary Indiana, Mrs. Edith Christiansen of Billings Montana, Mrs. Alice Doty of rural route 1 Brazil, Indiana Two sisters, Mrs. Anna Mitchell of Chicago and Mrs. Clyde Ruth of

Wichita Kansas. Two brothers Oliver and Ralph Sparks of Missouri. The body was brought to the Thomas Funeral Home and returned to the residence of the son. Funeral services will be held at the Christian church in South Fontanet Sunday afternoon with burial in Burnett cemetery.

A note: The farm girl remembers her grandmother died at the home of her uncle, David, and not at the grandmother's residence. Her grandmother did live alone in the home place until she became ill and went to stay with her son. Her uncle lived just down the road a piece from the farm girl.

Harvey William Cox - 72 years old died at his home on R R 1 Brazil, Indiana at 5 o'clock Wednesday morning. He is survived by the wife, Laura Virginia; one son, David, six daughters Flora Montague, Perrysville Ind; Ethel Scharf Gary, Indiana; Edith Christiansen Billings Montana, Alice Doty rural Brazil, Rose Westbrook Terre Haute and Eva Green in Mattoon Illinois. Three brothers, John L of Terre Haute, Frank of New Goshen, Walter of Rural Terre Haute and one sister Ida Lemons of Fontanet. The body was taken to Thomas Funeral home and will be returned to the residence of Mrs. Alice Doty. Brief funeral services will be held there at 1 o'clock Friday afternoon with continued services at the Christian church at South Fontanet. Burial will be in the Burnett Cemetery. Rev Eldon Meyers will have charge of the services assisted by Rev. Frank Agnew.

The farm girl remembers hearing her mother talk about Rev Agnew who was helpful when her grandparents were founders of the United Brethren Church in Fontanet. Probably the reason the services weren't held there is because the Christian church in South Fontanet was a more central location and it was before the UB congregation had built its church building. They probably considered it more proper and appropriate to have funerals in a church rather than the lower half of the lodge building in Fontanet where they held services.

With genealogical facts and stories to ponder, it reveals how all these ancestors lived and endured with perseverance to make each one today what they are. These people with their traits of being tall, short, thick or thin, blue or brown eyed, color of hair, humorous, beliefs, and talents have determined the characteristics for all the generations past, present and future.

BEING PATRIOTIC AT THE INDIANA ROOF AND DANCING

There were at least three military bases in the Indianapolis area during WWII and for several years. The patriotic thing to do was for young women to go to the Indiana Roof in Indianapolis to be dance partners for these men in uniform. It was a safe place for country girls to meet with strangers in a big city. There were soft drinks to buy and tons of free popcorn and pretzels. The Roof was beautiful with its wrought-iron balconies silhouetted against the ceiling designed like the starry skies. It was a replica of Chicago's Trianon or Aragon and attracted large crowds. There were live bands with singers. Middle-aged women were matrons who wore long black dresses and circulated on the dance floor to see that there was no hanky panky going on. Big men were bouncers in suits and black ties. If they spotted a bottle being sneaked out of a pocket didn't take long to confiscate the liquor and check it at the door to be picked up on the way out later. These country young women made a pact that they would always leave the Roof together. If during a dance someone suggested meeting afterward, they would say, "Well, there are five of us." Most of the time the answer would be, "Fine, let's meet across the street at that little restaurant." And if any young man had anything else on his mind, they would just disappear—the young man that is. Many friendships developed at the restaurant across the street that was open until at least 2 A.M. A few times some of the young men were invited to homes for Sunday dinners of home grown fried chicken.

There were four regulars, The farm girl Norma Mae, Gertrude Johnson and the Smith sisters Jean and Margie and sometimes another would go along. These young women rode the bus from Terre Haute to Indianapolis but not as often after one of them got a car, a 1949 green Ford convertible with a tan canvas top. It looked pretty snazzy and very comfortable unless you sat in the back seat on a cold night. Because the door lacked more than an inch of closing all the way, the wind whistled in real good. Guess they were young and didn't think to stuff paper or a towel in the gaping slit to block out the cold air. The canvas top flapped in the wind always so those in the back needn't worry what they said because those in the front couldn't hear above the car's top noise. It was worth the winter hardships to enjoy the cool breezes in the summertime. There wasn't much traffic on the Sunday mornings around 2 or 3 as they drove west on US 40 from Indianapolis to the rural drop off points in Fontanet and Sandcut and Burnett. where the Smith sisters lived. Pitching in for gas was cheaper than four or five bus tickets.

One night, or early morning, the carload was asleep except the driver, they thought. When Jean realized she didn't remember anything after she went through the stop lights in Brazil, she knew she could drive in her sleep. From that time on, it was required that at least one who sat in the front seat had to stay awake to keep her awake. She wanted someone just to talk. One night it was Gertrude's time to stay awake and instead of talking, she sang all the way from Indianapolis, and sang the same song. Being polite Jean didn't interrupt her singing but she is still talking about how annoyed she was. She can't remember what the song was except it was a popular song so guess she just blocked it out. A couple years later the convertible went from bad to worse and needed trading in and the car dealer was amazed at the lack of rubber barely covering the tire threads. It was a wonder those bald tires didn't blow out 5000 miles before.

A NORWEGIAN FRIEND AND GREAT OLD UNCLE

People other than men in service and young women went to the Indiana Roof. One of these five regulars worked at Commercial Solvents and there was a young man from Norway, whose father owned a similar company. He came to learn about the USA operation. He had the misfortune to arrive without luggage that somehow didn't get off the boat with him. For several days he wore the same clothes of tan pants and matching work-like tan shirt and even became quite crumpled looking. The company had several dinners and dances for various reasons and they were held in the Terre Haute House. Einer's luggage finally arrived in time for his dressy dark suit and bow tie to be worn to one of these festive events. There was a wonderful band, The Leo Baxter Swing Band. The Fontanet farm girl and Einer had become friends. She showed Einer how to jitterbug and it was great fun. When a waltz was played, Einer beamed at a dance he was most familiar. She acted reluctant to accept his invitation even though she could dance the waltz because she knew he would be the more experienced being from Norway. He said, "Oh come now I teach you as you did me the jitterbug." He and his partner, who was wearing a bright red dress with bare shoulders in the halter-top and wide bias skirt and high heels, soon caught the rhythm of the waltz and those on the Terre Haute House crowded floor stood alongside the walls as the couple danced and they could have won a prize. It was probably because Einer made an impression from being in the tan work clothes everyone had seen him, to the handsome young man in his well-tailored dark suit.

The Norwegian captured the friendship of most if not all the 800 who worked at Commercial Solvents and was included in parties and people invited him to their homes.

The Fontanet girl thought Einer would like the Indiana Roof and set the date for him to go with the group of four or five that regularly went to Indianapolis on Saturday nights and said they would meet at the bus station. Somehow they missed the bus and rather than be disappointed, Einer soon had a plan even though he knew her car was pretty old. He said, "You drive your car. I am mechanical engineer and I be perfect gentleman." So off they went in the two-door 1940 Chevy with no problems. Einer liked the Roof and was impressed with the live band and its variety of dance music. It was very foggy to have to drive home and she was glad it was a four lane highway. They followed a semi all the way from Plainfield to Terre Haute where the fog wasn't quite as dense where she dropped Einer off and then drove back the 14 miles to the little farm.

Later Einer bought a car to get him around, a Jeep-like vehicle. He was used to driving on the left and often ran over street curbs on the right. He was curious about American customs and asked questions. One evening there was a wiener roast planned at Deming park. He was noticed looking at a marshmallow, turning it over and over and then tasting the powdered coating. His eyes lit up, he frowned in wonder, and in his brisk dialect, he asked, "Marshmallow? Is it cake, is it candy?" As he was taking the farm girl home on a pitch black night he asked, "And what are those lights? They go on and they go off." Wondering what he was seeing, she told him she didn't see any lights. He said, "Oh, yes there are hundreds of them. The little lights go on and the lights go off.." She figured out it was lightning bugs or fireflies he was seeing.

The radio was playing and during an advertisement the announcer said, "And there are hundreds of bald men and women in the USA..." Einer asked, "Bald men and women. Does that mean unmarried?" And she didn't learn how to spell it but he told her Norwegian's Yea Elska Day. A few months later her aunt's husband who was born in Denmark came to visit. When she saw him she said, "Uncle Emil! Yea Elska Day...." No one knew what she had said but he smiled and came over and gave her a big Danish hug. She had told him, "Uncle Emil, I love you."

There was a great uncle (her mother's uncle Ollie) who came from Nevada, Missouri often to visit the family on the farm. He was a retired doctor and always had the latest car. He came once in a green Pontiac convertible that had chrome long horns on each side of the hood. He liked to travel and told when he sometimes took a carload of nurses to New Orleans. He liked to be chauffeured and would soon show his great niece all the gadgets on these new cars, where the clutch was or how to use the automatic gearshift and how to turn on the lights and then gave her the key to keep until he left. He was delighted to learn about the Indiana Roof and eager to take her friends in his new convertible with one rule: no one could smoke. When he realized he had left his false teeth in a cup at his brother and sister in law's when he stopped overnight in Chillicothee, Missouri before bringing them with him to the Indiana farm, he didn't want to go. The girls convinced Uncle Ollie he would look OK with or without his teeth. He was a slight-built man and without teeth looked all the more so. The Indiana Theater was below the Indiana Roof. The retired doctor was standing in line to get tickets for the Roof and an usher asked if he was in the wrong line. Didn't he need to be in the theater line? Didn't take long for that usher to be enlightened. The doctor and his carload sat at a table close to the band and the cute singer made the toothless doctor feel very debonair as she smiled and came to take him by the hand on stage to serenade him with a song. He danced with each one at the table and insisted they stay til the best dance, the last dance. Retired doctors from Missouri didn't live sixty years in this world for nuthin!

MISSED THE TITANIC – MARRIED SIXTY YEARS

The Danish uncle that had been told Yea Elska Day had a story to tell. When a young man, his country of Denmark was overtaken by Germany. His brother had already come to America and he wanted to do the same. He had his ticket bought and would have come on the Titanic except at the last minute he delayed his voyage so he could spend Easter with his mother. He had been stripped of his citizenship as Danish and was forced to be German. He did come after the Titanic sunk and entered the USA through Ellis Island. He said he had a little money but even a wiener sandwich cost twenty-five cents and he was glad when he was reunited with his brother.

He was 18 when he met Indiana-born Edith Cox in a Great Falls Montana hospital, where he was a janitor. Edith was in nurse training in Chicago before she accepted responsibility to go to Montana to help out during a flu epidemic. These young people both had remarkable compassion and wisdom. He wanted to help his beloved native country and his new country in the war against Germany, so he enlisted. He and Edith were married in 1917 one hour before he left with his regiment for New York... Edith borrowed money from her father that he sent by Western Union so she could go to New York with her new husband for one afternoon together before he left by sea in WWI. Since he was forced to be a citizen of Germany when Denmark was taken over, by law his bride became a German citizen. He served two years in the Army in France as a medical corpsman and eight months in the Argonne where many soldiers lost their lives or were wounded. Edith tried to follow him as a nurse but wasn't allowed to because only single women were accepted for overseas posts. While he was in France he received his American citizenship and his wife was glad to be an American again. After the war he borrowed a set of correspondence books from the farm girl's father and studied so he could pass a test to be a railroad postal clerk. This job provided a good living for his wife and their three children in Montana. The wife missed her Indiana family. She was thought to be courageous when she drove their 1927 Essex back home to Indiana with two small children. They put an ad in the newspaper asking if someone wanted a ride from Montana to Indiana. It isn't known if they were being generous, if they needed some fare money, or if they wanted another adult with Edith. A school teacher answered the ad and after they became acquainted, decided she would ride along to Iowa for a month and then be picked up again to go back to Montana. Bet she didn't know that in North Dakota going back, the Essex would somehow veer off the paved Highway 10, out into a field for several hundred feet before it stopped. Didn't seem to ruffle or fluster the driver as she backed the Essex up a little and managed to maneuver it back onto the highway. No one knew how that happened and they were glad nothing was damaged and they made it back to Montana just fine. The family didn't continue any friendship with the lady school teacher and it was probably her choice. During the many months and years apart, the Indiana daughter wrote letters often and almost monthly, slipped in a few dollars which helped her folks a lot.

This couple celebrated a 70th Wedding Anniversary in Billings Montana and they shared their philosophy for a happy marriage. If there is a misunderstanding, always talk it over. This Danish German American uncle was a loving husband, a gentle father, and an active member of the United Methodist Church, a member of the Masonic Lodge and Scottish Rite. He was also very involved with

Toastmasters Club.... And it was on a stopover from Montana to a convention in Washington DC that he visited Edith's family in Indiana. That is where his niece said, "Uncle Emil! Yea Elska Day." Wonder how many times he said that to his wife. He missed the Titanic and he didn't live in this world for nuthin.

A GREAT JOB WITH WONDERFUL PEOPLE

The 1945 junior girl's job at Commercial Solvents Corporation, commonly referred to as CSC, was pleasant and not boring. She used her bookkeeping skills to record vials of penicillin as they were counted off the assembly line. She accounted for the number of vials that were packaged in various lot numbers and it had to match the shipping department inventory. Because of all the chemicals made there, often there was a distinctive odor that made one standout when were in an elevator downtown. When people looked at you funny you either ignored them or said "it smells like bread and butter" and you would jingle the money in your pocket because the pay was good.

There was an office in one corner of the big manufacturing building with the penicillin department superintendent and secretary desks and some files. The secretary desk was an oak one with a center sloped section where the typewriter was stored when not in use. Most of the time she needed her desktop to do bookkeeping. This made it very uncomfortable with not being able to sit close to the desk or to put knees under. She had asked the department superintendent to get her another desk but he kept putting it off. One day the plant superintendent came and she asked him to please sit down at her desk. He did and then she said, "Pull yourself up closer so you can sit at the desk." He looked at her bewildered and put his hands on the desk front and pulled himself until his knees hit the typewriter storage with a bang, probably giving him bruises. He didn't say a word but that afternoon the trucking crew brought a big walnut desk with ample knee room and space for a typewriter on the right side. Through the eleven remaining years she worked there she went from various departments. Somehow she managed to have the truck drivers follow her with the beautiful walnut desk and when she became secretary to the same plant superintendent when he became the plant manager, sure enough she arrived with the walnut desk. On a really bad February morning the secretary was the first to make ruts in a deep snow from Fontanet to Terre Haute. There were drifts and she managed to drive through them making the fourteen miles pretty good until she reached the parking lot. As she tried to turn into an empty space, the car slid and sank into a big snowbank. She left the keys in the car and carefully crossed the icy street to her office building. She made a telephone call to the maintenance department to ask for help. The plant manager looked out the window and said, "Will you look at the parking lot! There is my highest priced plumber and two electricians pushing my secretary's car out of the snowdrift. I can't afford her." He was a sensitive boss and told her that when weather was this bad, he wanted her to stay home and be safe. There were several winter days she didn't brave blizzardy days but stayed safe at home on the farm.

Wonderful people worked at Commercial Solvents. The heart of the company was the main plant front gate where the watchman was headquartered in a red brick structure about ten feet square. Across the walkway was the reception room that had the latest modern switchboard. Calls within the departments of the three plants in various locations in Terre Haute could be dialed direct. Incoming calls lit up the switchboard and the long cords were connected to the holes for the called party. The operator pulled back a brass lever so it would ring and the light stayed on till they hung up and when the lights went off, both cords were pulled. The board was big and most of the time there were two operators. Thelma Hart and Helen Jackson were operators several years. Phones inside the plants could dial locally outside. Outside calls coming in had to be handled manually on the switchboard. The operators had to handle long distance and conference calls between the several plants in the U.S. and to the corporate offices in New York. Helen became close friends with the Fontanet girl and included her as an attendant in her wedding. Helen was a beautiful bride and her attendants wore light weight faille-like dresses with cinched waists and full skirts over hoops. The maid of honor's was blue and the two bridesmaids wore yellow. The friendship continued and thirty years later the farm girl and her daughter, Linda, visited Helen in San Jose California to enjoy sightseeing in San Francisco, driving along the Pacific Ocean and visiting Clint Eastwood's famous Hog's Breath in Carmel. Linda said dinner there would be her treat and later said she wanted the charge to show on her credit card as a token of being there even though Clint wasn't there.

At CSC there were men who were truck drivers, men and women who worked in production of making penicillin which was discovered from the mold off discarded corn mash from making whiskey. There were several packaging lines with girls in white uniforms and paper snoods covering their hair, as the various forms of penicillin were bottled and labeled. There were scientists that did research and quality control. There were secretaries and bosses and lots of friendships of many employees formed and kept for years. One Wednesday evening before the four-day Thanksgiving Holiday, one newly employed young woman looked a little lonely at the gate waiting for the bus. The farm girl, realizing the new secretary had just come from England, asked her what her plans were for her first Thanksgiving in America. The foreign girl was befriended and asked to the farm in the country. Apologizing that the dinner tomorrow wouldn't be the traditional turkey, dressing, mashed potatoes, cranberry-kind, said she would be welcome to the oyster stew and pumpkin pie dinner at her aunt's. Tradition wasn't an issue with the English friend and she enjoyed a wonderful weekend on the farm getting acquainted with parents and aunts and uncles and cousins. This English girl visited in the home often and remained in the hearts of the family on the farm. Her customs were shared and found quaint in her new American environment. Once she marveled that butter was available with every meal in a restaurant. A young Fontanet girl had died and her host family stopped on the way home from church at the funeral home to pay their respects. The English girl was amazed at the sweetness of the little girl in the casket with her doll and the beautiful flowers in the room. She was hesitant to go in but was glad she did and realized it was a sweet sorrow. In England she was accustomed to a simpler laying out of bodies.

It was sad for her when the father in the home where she visited, suddenly had a heart attack and died. It meant a lot to her to know what to expect at the funeral home as she attended the visitation and funeral for her comfort and to be of comfort to the farm family. It seemed very unusual in January and February to have so many severe thunderstorms in Indiana. She stayed a lot with the rest of the family during that winter and they felt safer with her there. It is a big wide world and customs shared with friendships, no doubt is pleasing to the God who created the Earth and all its population.

Commercial Solvents had yearly Christmas parties for employees and their families. It was usually held at Indiana State University in the gym. One year the gifts for kids were a disaster. There weren't enough and eleven-year-old boys got sets of toy dishes or thirteen-year old girls got dump trucks. The secretary mentioned to the Plant Manager that she thought there could be a better way to get toys more suitable. He said, "Ok, you do it!" She didn't expect that but accepted the challenge. She used a list of employees from Personnel and sorted them by departments. She listed the names on a survey sheet with columns for them to write whether their children were boys or girls with their ages. She tallied them and had a committee to help her choose gifts. She rounded the number of each group to buy to the next nearest dozen. The presents were wrapped by Schultz Toy Dept and swatches of paper put in a notebook so the boy ages and girl ages could be identified by its wrapping. At the next Christmas party there were roped lines and signs and kids were happy with an appropriate gift. This project expanded and she did it for a CSC plant in Sterling Louisiana. She sent the surveys and purchased the gifts that were shipped down there.

Holiday Season 1955 the farm girl was helping plan the CSC party and volunteered to sing in the chorus for the program. She remembers it may have been Jack Roman who assumed the position of director. Not enough men signed up so she mentioned it to her dad. He brightened up and said he sure would like to sing and he went to the two rehearsals and sang the night of the employees and families party in the big Indiana State gym. They needed a singer for the opening The Lord's Prayer and there was a college student, who also happened to be related. Linda Doty agreed to sing and she had a voice the farm girl was proud to have recommended. It was a gala occasion and the farm girl didn't know that her father would suddenly pass away in about three weeks and this night would be another sweet memory.

After these parties any extra gifts were stored and given the next Christmas to the Rose Orphans' home. She asked the house parents for names and ages and made name labels to match a gift and the children were delighted.

She left CSC to be married and she moved to Illinois to raise a family. The plant manager wrote a letter of reference for her that was fit to be framed with comments of praise she never expected.

IT'S GREEK TO ME AT EASTERN ILLINOIS UNIVERSITY

The Fontanet farm girl's husband was the head of the electrical maintenance department at Eastern Illinois University. She had enjoyed the university community and was acquainted with several by attending various dinners of recognition and picnics. Many dances were held in the ballrooms. Her husband liked to polka and he would say, "Come on Norma Mae, let's do the Sigel Hop." She had heard him say that in his younger days, he liked to go to the little town of Sigel sorta south and west of Mattoon to dance.

After his death in 1986, she missed the university atmosphere and was glad she was accepted for a position in the Student Life office as secretary for Greek Life. During the interview she was given a Greek Week booklet that had descriptions of what the system was about. In it was the Greek alphabet with the symbols she'd often seen in front of the sorority and fraternity houses or on sweatshirts. Seemed terribly complicated and she was surprised and scared when she was offered the job. It was "all Greek" to her until she learned that being Greek meant being a member of a fraternity or sorority chapter that use Greek alphabet letters for identification. Alpha Gamma Delta would be A Γ Δ or Sigma Chi would be ΣX. A is Alpha and Ω is Omega. Other chapters were Alpha Phi, Alpha Sigma Alpha, Alpha Sigma Tau, Delta Delta Delta, Delta Zeta, Kappa Delta, Sigma Kappa and Sigma Sigma Sigma sororities. Fraternities were Delta Chi, Delta Sigma Phi, Delta Tau Delta, Lambda Chi Alpha, Phi Kappa Theta, Pi Kappa Alpha, Sigma Nu, Sigma Phi Epsilon, Sigma Pi and Tau Kappa Epsilon. The job was not boring and she worked with hundreds of fraternity and sorority chapter members. She attended many banquets and anniversary celebrations of the chapters. She heard motivational speeches. She admired the sincere recognition of accomplishment for community service or academic excellence. She respected the young men and young women as their chaplains led prayer for the occasions. She was respected by the students probably because she was the mother or grandmotherly type and working with these students kept her young and she never felt old. She was at ease when she accompanied fifty or more new members on a bus for an overnight retreat. She participated in discussions, mostly listening and occasionally interjecting an idea. She learned a lot. They were awesome weekends and she found that most issues were not confined to age or gender but typical to apply to everyone. She appreciated the excitement to wear a glitzy dress to Greek Sing competition, or an Awards banquet. At one Valentine formal she assumed the role to make it fun for everyone. She mingled with students at tables or groups standing along the wall. She picked out couples and took them by the hand to the dance floor. She took others and joined hands with them in the circle dances. She wondered if she had ever been young and shy. She didn't remember having to sit and watch others dance!

She was often asked questions either on the phone or ones who came to her desk. When asked, "Which sorority do you think is the best one for my daughter?" "Which is the best one on campus?" Her honest reply would be, "Each sorority is unique in its own way and they each have similar founded beliefs." She also advises parents to be interested in their student's choice and learn about the experience and be supportive. She was often asked, "Is any sorority or fraternity 'in trouble?" Again, she could say that any fraternity or sorority who is participating in chapter membership recruitment, has to be in good standing with the university and the Greek Life Office. And even if a chapter has experienced problems, it could be the better one because of local or national headquarter intervention and steps taken to solve the problems with new programs to strengthen the chapter. Truth is, she really loves all the chapters and the officers and members. She feels with them like she does her children – she will always talk about the good things they do, but never when they are in trouble. She is saddened when they do misbehave and she takes joy with the community service and fun things they do. One of her cousins when he learned that she worked with the Greeks, sent her an almost letter of sympathy that she had to do that. He no doubt, had hang-ups about stories of criticism of fraternities and the movie, Animal House. She thinks it is too bad that the antics of some, label all. The farm girl was quick to reply to her cousin, "My Greeks are Angels!" And she pondered that if all chapters went by the fundamental rituals of the founders, returning to basics, her Greeks could be Angels... and if not now, someday they will be.

She can still smile as she explains to those who say, "Oh you work with the Greeks in sororities and fraternities." And she further said, "There are more than 1500 or so students each semester." They will remark they didn't realize there were so many students from Greece. She has explained many times the students are not from Greece, but belong to chapters that use letters from the Greek alphabet. Until they ask and learn, it is also Greek to them. Often in her office she would have telephone calls from parents concerned that their son or daughter was considering joining a Greek organization. Questions like, "Which is the best fraternity and are they going to do this and that." She was serious with the answers, and explained that the chapters are made up with diverse students and the chapters change from time to time as it reflects the efforts of the members. She explains the opportunities for students to be chapter officers and involvement with committees. She hopes the chapters are emphasizing academic excellence, etc. She has often explained further that nothing should be said or done that would be offensive or considered hazing. To do so would be against the laws of Illinois, the statutes of the university, the offices of national headquarters, and strictly enforced by the Office of Greek Life. Always ending on positive notes of parents becoming involved to learn and be anxious to participate in Parent Days of the chapter their sons and daughters might become members.

A wonderful surprise and tribute was offered her to become an honorary member of the Alpha Theta chapter of the Order of Omega. As she participated in the candle ceremony of induction, she felt so humble and honored to realize she was an honorary member of the organization that includes the top 2% of sorority and fraternity chapter members. Juniors and seniors submit their application which lists qualifications of leadership and academic ability for membership in this prestigious Greek-lettered national organization. She proudly wears her Omega pin and displays her framed membership certificate. After many years in the Greek Life Office, it isn't "Greek to Her" anymore. Yearly she was honored with an Appreciation Day.

One year the Greek Week Committee got the idea in February and each chapter made a quilt block with their letters and a greeting. They had it professionally quilted. The secret was kept until it was presented to her in April at the Awards Banquet at the end of Greek Week. It is a coveted item and often used in one of her bedrooms as a spread. She entered it in the Coles County Fair in a category, Quilt with a Story, and it won a blue ribbon first prize!

Norma Mae Doty Taylor

    One year she wrote a poem and it reflected back to her roots in the Fontanet school in Indiana.

APPRECIATION DAY

As many thoughts often go through my head
I decided to write so you can read what I've said.
It's time for another Norma Taylor Appreciation Day.
An opportunity for me, a few more things to say.

Sometimes as I sort through applications for rush
I often wonder, will this one excel in grades, add as much
To the Fraternity/Sorority System as past and present officers,
Be a chapter president and a role model in their office?

You see, many years ago, when I was in high school
Not always, but most of the time I went by the rules.
It was way back... way back in Year.. Year one,
I managed to make some A's, along with the fun.

In Fontanet, Indiana, the school had grades 1 thru 12
The mother of a 6th grader told my mother and she me, did tell,
"Every night when Shirley comes home from school, I soon know
every thing that Norma does, and what she wears from head to toe."

I was pleased that this little Shirley Branam had chosen me.
I dressed with care, made sure my hems were below the knee
And I sort of quieted down, didn't so much act the fool,
Knowing that I was a role model for those at school.

Sad news cast a spell at school after one Thanksgiving break.
More than a holiday feast had caused Shirley's tummy ache;
Appendicitis was the case. She 's not looking up to me any more
But looking down from Heaven, her influence on me forever more.

My ego was boosted to know someone respected me
And I watched that the best in me she would see.
As I think about this to relate to My Appreciation Day,
I hope there is a message somewhere along the way.

When there are those that you admire, let them be aware
And let them know their influence abounds everywhere.
And to my fraternity/sorority friends, if something I do or say
Helps you along the way, then I humbly accept this Appreciation Day.

The farm girl became acquainted with many of the administrators, staff and students at Eastern Illinois University. It was her privilege to meet them on campus and know them by name and be pleased to hear them say, "Hi, Norma." She was flattered that many who moved on to advanced jobs or graduated, kept in touch with her and she hopes they won't forget her. She will always remember the ones in Greek advisory positions. Sherrie was the first and was so patient to teach her "Greek" terminology of sororities and fraternities in her new role of Secretary Greek Life. The farm girl remembers feeling really lost to be back to work again, so soon after her husband had passed away, and after several years she had been "just" a housewife. Being busy with lots of typing to do, and being with these students, made her appreciate she had skills to rely on. The next was Eileen, introduced as Bean (by her nickname she will always affectionately be known). She was a student when the farm girl first met her and didn't know then that Eileen would graduate, go to Western Illinois University for her masters and then return to Eastern to be her boss. Another was Becky who came out of grad school from Michigan. The positions were Assistant Directors and in about three years these new professionals were eager to move on to higher positions. The farm girl applauds the EIU administrators for making the position one of Director. She thinks this will keep these qualified persons in the position and the students in the fraternities and sororities will get the benefit of their experience. Sherrie went on to a large campus and earned a doctorate degree. Eileen also pursued a doctorate and is vice president at a private college. Becky is a director in a large junior college and also working on a doctoral degree. The Greek Life and the Student Life are in the same office. She remembers directors Anita and the next one David. Their families were "office families" too. The closeness of all the ones working was unified with diversity appreciation. She was comfortable to call the university president by his first name, Lou, or a vice president, Shirley.

Norma Mae Doty Taylor

ODE TO BECKY MARUSHAK
By Norma

Becky, these three years really have just flown
And I think our friendship by each day has grown
From around an interview table, the first time we met
And hosting grueling questions, your answers to get.

The older we get the faster time goes by
And I'm Pretty Old, so the days did really fly!
I've written a poem or two before this one
But this is one where words are hard to come!

Just when we get to know more about you
And feel comfortable as a good old worn shoe
You've outgrown Assistant Director Student Life
It's now about time to say Good Bye!

May your next interview pay off with big money
As in new territory to Arizona you journey
May you find true happiness in that new land
With God having you in the palm of His Hands.

Someday when you, too, are wiser and old
Will you remember humorous and sad stories told
By those who really tried to teach you all we know?
And will you think fondly of the gang at EIU SLO?

ODE TO THE STUDENT LIFE OFFICE GANG
EASTERN ILLINOIS UNIVERSITY
(As seen through the trifocals of Norma Taylor)

Tis the last day of togetherness for 1999
For the staff in the EIU Office of Student Life
What Y2K will bring is yet to be seen
Let's reminisce how this past semester has been.

Ceci, You're great and have your hand on the helm
You steer this gang like a pro, me you overwhelm!
Fill that resume with all your many skills
And be the next SLO Director, not acting at will.

Bob, you've been Greek Advisor since July
I hope by now you're not wondering why!
Has it been as you expected, or anything more?
Have you performed duties that weren't a bore?

Thalia, you are the backbone of the Spirit of SLO
If it needs to be done or said, you always make it so!
You provide stability, experience and lots of advice
For 2000, I hope you will be wealthy, healthy and wise!

Who's left? Oh Yeah. The Greek Secretary, Norma
I'd like to think, without her things would not be normal.
Take note ALL, today she is wearing her Christmas sweater
And the Liz Clabourne red knit pants, good for the weather.

If we've got talents, and feelings to express, Let's all boast!
And if not actual, let's raise our glasses for a toast
May we all continue to do what we do best
And make 2000 the very best year yet!

A FATHER'S EXAMPLE

The farm girl's dad was a deep thinker and expressed his opinions verbally and in things he wrote. The following is exact copy of a story he wrote on yellow lined tablet paper in his good old fashioned handwriting:

"Story of the life and character of our Lord Jesus Christ.
To be read in memory of Him at this Christmas time.

The name Jesus signifies Jehovah is Salvation. The name Christ signifies anointed. Jesus was both King and Priest. The life and character of Jesus Christ is the holy of holies in the history of the world. Jesus left his home in Heaven and all the Glory of God and Angels to take a lowly place in the earth for the sole purpose of redeeming fallen humanity from sin and distruction.

Jesus mission was lowly and he became dispised, but yet this mission was too sacred to be intrusted even to the Holy Angels. God looked down from Heaven and behold! A Virgin praying; God honored her prayers and her virginity that he sent Gabriel the Arch Angel to announce to her that she was to become the mother of the Christ Child. He was born of the Virgin Mary. God being his Father.

At Bethleham of Judea, six miles south of Jerusalem, Jesus was born into this world at the darkest period of sin and error, to become the light of the world. At the time of Jesus birth the world was at peace and people were happy as it is to this date at Christmas time. Jesus having a manger for his cradle received a visit of adoration from the three wise men of the east. At fourty days old he was taken to the temple of Jerusalem and returning to Bethlehem, was soon taken to Egypt to escape Herod's massacre of the infants there. After a few months stay there the wicked King died. Then the family returned to their Nazareth home. Jesus was thus called a Nazarene. Jesus lived at Nazareth until he was about thirty years old subject to his parents care, increasing in wisdom and stature and in favor with God and man.

His childhood home country was rugged and mountainous, filled with natural scenery and beauty, blessed with pure air, and clear cool springs.

Jesus first school was his home. His first teacher his parents at the age of five or six years he entered the elementary school. Perhaps the first lesson he learned in school was the Creed of Deuteronomy 6:4 "Hear O Israel the Lord our God is one Lord," and other passages of scripture such as Psalm 114, 118 and 136. At this early date it was profusely said that the world is only saved by the breath of school children. Even the Christ-child was taught the necessity and beauty of reciting his daily prayers. Besides all this Jesus no doubt learned the carpenter's trade with his parent Joseph and may have contributed to the support of his mother.

Jesus attended his first Passover at the age of twelve years. He was so filled with the wisdom of God that he astonished learned men in the temple.

He was baptized by John the Baptist in the river Jordan in A.D. twenty-seven with the Holy Spirit in the form of a dove descending upon him. Putting his faith in God and trusting always in prayer, Jesus willingly accepted the great task of bringing salvation to all mankind. Immediately he went about choosing men who were willing to help him, twelve in all were chosen. He called them Disciples. Jesus personally instructed and trained the disciples in the ways of truth and righteousness according to the plan of God.

Jesus went about throughout all his life in this world doing good for the whole human family. He healed the sick, restored sight to the blind, made the lame walk and raised men from the dead. He was so pure that he put forth his hand and touched a poor miserable lepper and immediately the lepper was healed. He did many other miricles. So great is his power that the sea and a mighty wind obayed his voice."

The above story to be read at Christmas is copied including the few misspelled words. to immortalize the words written on the yellow lined tablet many years ago, and as a tribute to the man who moved his family to the country to be a farmer and a neighbor and was a charter member of the Fontanet United Brethren Church.

The farm girl's father stood straight and tall, looked taller than his 5 feet 11 inches with dark brown dyes. His mannerism was outgoing and he sorta leaned his head to the right before he would say something. He was a proud man and his Sunday clothes had to be the best and he wore the one Hart, Shaffner and Marx dark blue serge suit until it was shiny. It was the only suit anyone could remember but it always looked stylish until his waist went from 28 to 29 inches and he bought a light bluish gray suit. His shoes had to be from Hanover's in Terre Haute.

Little did he know his story would prove that he didn't live sixty years in this world for nuthin.

LOVE! LOVE A BEAUTIFUL FEELING

Love is in the air. In Spring a young man's fancy turns to love. When fresh green sprouts of grass emerge, when a crocus blooms through the snow, when the bleats of newborn lambs can be heard, when the days get longer after a cold winter, when the sun melts the snow, Spring is in the air. Love is in the air.

Love in the air is an atmosphere, but the degree of love is mentally and physically felt. Felt deep in the heart, mind and soul of the one who grew from the 1945 high school junior with white powdered hair in the class play, to the sixty-year-old woman with naturally aged white hair who has a story. She knows the feeling of love. She feels love as a pressure within her chest, or a warm feeling within her heart. Knowing the Love of God, the Love of her Savior Jesus Christ, permeates to the utmost in the bottom of her heart. All other loves form accordingly. Love of parents, love of spouse, love of children. God's perfect plan for the happy family are those with the experience of God's Love, love and respect of parents, and a loving husband and wife who follow God's word to cleave to one another, forsaking all others. While still loving and respecting parents, the degree of love should flourish under God between the husband and wife. Lucky are the children in this pattern. With parents who love God and one another, parents' capacity for loving children is as deep and wide as possible. When parents put the love of children above the love of their spouse, the wheel of love is unbalanced and some will fall off along the way.

Remembering the first songs in Sunday School. "Jesus Loves Me, This I know." What would it mean if it said Jesus Likes me.... Or the difference of a mother loving her child or a mother liking her child, The difference of a father loving his son or liking him. If parents love their children and like them too, especially after the terrible twos and the perplexing teen years... She would say this with humor to illustrate perfect relationships of unconditional love

When new food is first tasted it might be rated ok, or good or wonderfully delicious. Some might even say they love it. That's the degree of pleasure found in the food. The farm girl believes at first we may just like it and then a taste is developed where we might realize we love it, and we get hungry for it, have a craving for it. Our growth of love can be compared. So should it be with our relationship with God. We need to be hungry for His word as much as we feel our craving for a delicious food.

Jesus was hung on a cross to shed His blood. He suffered and was the ultimate sacrifice by His father who showed the ultimate Love for all mankind. Jesus offered a prayer to His Father God that those who persecuted Him be forgiven. Followers are those who through the centuries, have accepted the Word of God and accepted the Son Jesus, as Savior and have the Spirit within.

Growing up with parents who are loving and caring, instills traits in kids that last forever.

Being taught that God is Love, singing songs that Jesus Loves Me, and saying prayers lays a foundation for the lucky kids. Spending time with children as they say "Now I Lay me Down to Sleep, I pray the Lord my soul to Keep, Thy Love guard me through the Night, And wake me with the morning Light" is beautiful as the day ends and assuring to look forward to the next.

Memorizing verses from the Bible like John 3:16 "For God so loved the world that he gave his only begotten Son, that whosoever believeth in him should not perish, but have everlasting life" and believing it, is the acceptance of God's promise. The ultimate degree of love between a father and son and for the children of God. The ultimate degree! Forgiven and forgiving lifts weights of burdens. Allowing burdens to be lifted actually cleanses the heart from ill feelings and guilt, making space for happy thoughts and positive planning. Showing others the Love, brightens corners. The farm girl believes that helping others as she has been helped demonstrates that God works through his followers. Prayers should be that we know what God's plan for us is. When the plan is known, the plan can be worked.

When anyone attempts to solve their problems, to do what they want to do, do their own will, WITHOUT knowing the love of GOD and the power and changes within themselves with prayer, NO PLAN WILL WORK to the best advantage. How does one without a plan for where they are going, know when they get there?

When committed to accepting the love of God and humbling to his Will, answers will come for problems. Who can function in harmony with themselves or others when burdened with doubts, disbeliefs, or ill feelings. These are lifted with prayer, "I am in need of help...and like the psalmist, my help cometh from the Lord."

And things happen with God working through others. The farm girl believes when what we want or our plans don't work, we learn to accept it is not God's Will and a better way will be provided. Often situations reach a bottom and then there is no other way but up. When doors are closed, others open. And each of us have the choice.... We can forgive and be forgiven of anything that separates us from the Will of God.... Empty our hearts and accept being filled with the peace of having a Savior by our side. So simple it is to prayerfully ask, "Let me release anything that separates me from God's will." Like when the farm girl was 14, the opportunity was given to say, "Just as I am, I come." She grew with faith. She truly learned to love and be loved beyond any love she had ever known.

She believes that when filled with the Love of God, the intense feeling is felt in our hearts. The capacity to love and be loved is unending. And to love ourselves is not an ego, but our commitment to those we love, that we allow ourselves to be loveable

As in the Bible 1 John 4:12, "If we love one another, God dwelleth in us, and His love is perfected in us." She believes if foremost we do love one another, doesn't mean we have to agree or condone. His love within us sheds the light for us to work through the darkness of concern. His love and our prayer while seeking wisdom, will make a difference how we react.

The Word of God was, is and will be the same. If through the centuries, God had allowed His word to be changed, even the Ten Commandments would not be recognized or relevant. Yesterday, today and tomorrow, God's Word is the yardstick for stability and hope. God's Word is the Truth. His children make the choices to stay within the Word or stray so far they nearly fall or do fall over the bounds of safety. The way back is to acknowledge the need for forgiveness. The man who has said, "As for me and my house, we shall serve the Lord," has worked within the family to provide his children a Yardstick of Values. When children stray so far, have broken parent hearts, rebelled, brought problems they can't handle, and disregarded what they were taught, they have made choices. Should children expect parents to accept their rebellion, and disrespect? The farm girl believes the parents should not lessen the Yardstick. Let the children know they are still loved unconditionally but let children know they are the ones who severed or damaged the relationship by their choice. Doesn't mean ideas can't be changed but not without careful study. Word of God or values should be taken very seriously and respected. Any interpretation must not stray from the Word nor be a compromise. New ideas and concepts on issues, other than Bible substantiated, make one grow and adds new dimensions of excitement.

If variances or deviation from one's good upbringing sway too far, after one or more generations the farm girl believes there would soon be no Yardstick of Values with which to measure. Instead of lightly wielding or yielding to adverse beliefs, holding firm is a way of preserving interpretations of right and wrong. Instead of bending down, she believes it is better to stand tall and reach out in love to bring others up rather than to be pulled down.

FONTANET BEAN DINNER

The school band played at the Fontanet Bean Dinner. The Bean Dinner was started by a small group of Civil War veterans as a reunion to remember the days of war and to celebrate being back home. A big black pot of navy beans was cooked over hickory wood served with crackers to symbolize the crude food and hard tack. This tradition became annual and grew until eventually there were 11 big black iron pots of beans cooked (2200 pounds of beans) with bacon. The fire is started at 5 A.M. and the beans are cooked to serve at noon. Long lines are formed and the beans dipped to the Bean Dinner goers. 4Hers raise money by having a stand that sells cornbread. Politicians have tents to provide cold water for visitors and opportunity to pass out cards and talk about issues. Carnival rides were added and a live band plays for dancing in a constructed cement pavilion with a roof. Two lines start forming about 10:30 and it is good to have more than one person so one can stand in line and the other can go up and down the lines to see who of several generations are there. If you don't know someone you don't hesitate to ask who they are and where they live. It is not unusual for politicians to visit these lines to hand out cards or rulers asking for votes. Some are greeted with nods, handshakes and others with big neighborly hugs. The now adult farm girl was so glad to see the little neighbor boy who was all grown up and running for another term as a state representative. She was suddenly reminded that when he was little and one of the Kersey neighbor kids, she had heard him talking often to his imaginary friends, Jimmy and Shimmy. Now she thinks he was practicing a speech for when he would be in Indianapolis representing the people of the Fontanet area.

Sixty Years in This Wicked World for Nuthin

There are those who remember when having 25 cents to spend at the Bean Dinner was great. Probably would buy an ice cream cone and tickets for the merry go round. The farm girl's father worked for the Pennsylvania Railroad and had access to scrap lumber. He hauled old box car doors home and built hog houses and added a kitchen to the original house. He also drew plans and built a new outhouse. It was far ahead of its day with the bench having two adult holes and a lower bench with a kid-size hole. Many years later a cousin confessed that they loved to come to Uncle Grover's and they thought he was rich because he had such a wonderful outhouse. There were iron hardware hinges and clasps on the boxcar doors that had to be taken off. The farm girl was about nine years old and she learned to take a crowbar and take out the bolts that held the hinges. She threw the iron pieces in a pile until they could be loaded in the old black Chevy and her dad could sell them at the scrap salvage place. One summer she had 75 cents to spend at the Bean Dinner.

One certain member of the Fontanet class of 1946 prided herself that she had never missed a Bean Dinner. She was three weeks old when her parents carried her a mile and a half to show her off. On the 90th Anniversary of the Bean Dinner, this 1946er rolled down her car window to pay the $1 fee to park the car inside the grounds. As she handed the attendant her dollar, she proudly announced that "she had never missed a bean dinner." The young man looked at her and said, "But my, my, you sure look good for 90..." The farm girl went many more years to the Bean Dinner but she didn't make any more announcements when paying her dollar to park.

To continue the sparks of interest for the Bean Dinner, some new things needed to be added several years ago.

Just like the 4H Motto, she wrote a letter to the committee in charge, not to be critical but To Make the Best Better, and suggested that at noon just before the beans were served that the Grand Old Flag be raised and a bugler play Taps to commemorate the sacrifices of those in the Civil War who lost lives and as a tribute to all those who were standing in line to get beans to remember the meaning of why there was a bean dinner. She suggested that on Sunday morning there be a combined church service in the roofed dance pavilion. She thought carnival workers might like to attend. The suggestions were thought to be good. At a most recent Bean Dinner the church service was held at 10 a.m. and several close-by country churches participated. There was an hour of singing with special songs by two young teen girls, a man and his guitar, ladies accompanied by a keyboard and each beautiful and meaningful, with messages to churn your conscience and warm your heart. It was an inspirational service with singing "Amazing Grace" and "Precious Memories" and hearing a wonderful message of Heritages and Legacies. The slight breeze to make it comfortable and seeing puffs of smoke from the fires under pots of beans and smelling the hickory firewood as the flag was waving, is something no one should ever miss at the church service once a year at the Fontanet Bean Dinner usually on the last Sunday in August.

No wonder the basketball team was nicknamed Beantowners!

GOOD NEIGHBORS

Neighbors were the heart of a farm community. Houses were far apart that couldn't be seen but everyone knew that if anyone needed something, help was near. There were dinner bells too that if heard ringing at odd times and for a long time, it would get attention. Even at night, especially in the summer time when windows were open, yells or bells could be heard for miles around.

One neighbor's name was actually Judge Wells and he was called Jud. The farm girl's dad and he both had fox hounds. At night they would often sit together and listen to their dogs chasing a fox. They could tell which dog was ahead and the closest to the fox. It was kinda like a competition to see which one's dog was more aggressive on the trail that night. One of the best dogs that Jud had was named Gyp and her dad's dog was Boots. The fox hounds were also good to roust out rabbits during hunting season. These sports allowed a lot of time for visiting between these two neighbors and a friendship developed that even they didn't realize at the time.

Jud liked having fun and playing practical jokes. The neighbors got together at least once a month and usually in the new cottage farmhouse that had a big combined dining and living room. There were games they played especially the first time a new neighbor joined in. They would ask the player to sit on the floor with their feet straight out with their ankles apart. A half cup of water was put on the floor between their ankles and they were given two tablespoons and told to bend over to their ankles and hack through the water with the spoons The other player, the experienced player, would sit on the floor also with his feet straight ahead and parted at the ankles. He too would hit his spoons in the water. If the game had a name or purpose, no one ever figured out.

But as the two were hacking the water, the experienced player took ahold of the new player's feet and pulled him through the water. No wonder only new neighbors or visitors were invited to play this game.

At another party, the women made up a game. The prize would be a big mincemeat pie that only the winners of the game could eat while the losers had to watch. A women team and a men team competed and they had to use a man's tie and the first player had to put it around the neck and make two loops and undo it and pass it to the next player. The women were enthusiastic and "tried" real hard but the men won and were so anxious to cut the pie. The pie was just the right hue of brown and smelled scrumptious. It was cut in even slices of eight so each man could have his part of the prize. The first to eat a bite was quick to hide his astonishment to keep his mouth shut and to find a way to get outside without arousing suspicion. The next one to take a bite did the same. They were all good sports and wanted the others to feel the brunt also. Truth was the women had purposely let the men win the doctored pie. They had used salt instead of sugar. Egg shells that had been broken up and were drying on the warming oven of the baker's cook stove somehow got in the pie. All harmless even if ingested but not difficult to imagine what it would taste like and feel like. Question after that was, to be a winner or not to be a winner!

GROWING UP ON A LITTLE FARM

Living on a little farm provided experiences not possible any other way. There was seldom any extra money but always lots of good things to eat. Gardens were pictures of perfectly straight rows of green beans, carrots, potatoes, peas and onions. Beds of sprawling cucumber, muskmelon and watermelon vines were along the edges of the garden. The farm girl's mother always wanted two or three rows of zinnias and marigolds next to the road or driveway to beautiful the place. Flowers were tall and would last well into the frost season and hide the rest of the garden as it lost its magic and had weeds higher than the vegetables that had gone to seed. Her dad growled that it was too much hard work to plow and tend to anything other than something needed to eat. Somehow, when the seeding was done and the plants began to pop through the ground and make leaves, there were always two or three rows of flowers next to the road. Sometimes new flowers were added along with the "zinnies" and marigolds. One time there were cock's combs that resembled a rooster comb and the blooms were phenomenally big, measuring nine inches across and twelve or fourteen inches long. Cars would slow down to look at them or people walking would stop to see. Her dad was proud when they did and he was always first to pick a bouquet of zinnies to give away. They stood on a street corner in Terre Haute one time and sold the cock's combs for 25 cents apiece. These deep red velvety flowers looked real good hanging upside down on the wall or in a big vase.

Trees of yellow, red, blue and purple plums seemed just to sprout up. No one ever remembered planting these trees but everybody had them. People liked plums to eat and they made good jelly and pies. The chickens were fed the cooked skins from the jelly. The 4Hers liked plums and used a nut picker to prick the skins so they would stay whole in the cold packer and look colorful at the fair for their canning projects. Blackberries and wild raspberries provided the iron in diets and also made delicious pies. Country folk picked berries enough to can for their own family and for city kin who would be coming to visit. When the green beans and tomatoes were being canned, it was the same thing, so many quarts to get from one season to the next for the family and then add enough for the visitors.

With cows, pigs and chickens on the farm, milk and meat and eggs were available to make perfect meals. Nothing was better than coming in the house after an all day trip to town than a quick meal – of home-canned sausage in the oven and the drippings in a skillet for rich milk gravy, with browned slices of left-over baked potatoes. Cold biscuits retained their savor with the steaming gravy. A meal could never have been faster. No need for a McDonalds way back then.

When city folks visited country kin and sometimes stayed a week, they knew to take bags of sugar and flour. Wouldn't be long before cans of blackberries were opened and pies were in the oven. Grandkids remember how their grandmother sent them to the garden to pick peas or green beans. She would give them a bucket and tell them to fill it up to the top. The kids would fluff up the beans or peapods and never pack them down to get the buckets filled sooner. Actually grandma Cox would have been pleased if they had been half full. A lot of grandkids with buckets soon got the job done for enough to cook for the gang that was there for a meal. One time there were four cousins visiting grandma and were about four to six years old. They came in from playing and wanted something to eat. The grandma had just made bread and their aunt was fixing the yummy bread with jelly. One of these little boys had been shying away from his aunt and when he got near her, he would turn sideways and almost make a face at her. She made bread and jelly for Raymond, Hazel and her son Howard, and then looked at Hurley. She said, "Oh, Hurley you don't like me, do you?" He looked at the others with their jellied bread and again at her with his big brown eyes. After some hesitation he finally said, "Oh, Aunt Alice, I like you in the kitchen."

Country kids had chores to do which was just part of their day. Little kids had easy jobs and bigger kids had harder jobs. Kids looked forward to graduate from younger chores as they got older. A sign of success and maturity was going from carrying kindling to chopping wood or from washing fruit jars to help peel and pack jars. Each season had its own fascination. Kids could hardly wait for the threshing machines to come through to separate the grain from the straw as the cut wheat was brought on hay racks to the machine. Most beds had either straw or feathers in their heavy blue and white ticking. Kids liked helping mothers empty the ticks of the old straw and it was either put in the chicken house hens' nests or sometimes around the strawberry plants. The ticking was washed and hung on the line to dry and smelled country sunshine fresh. It was great fun to stuff new clean bright straw in the ticks. The farm girl remembers her ornate iron bed and its comfortable straw tick.

There were plenty of wonderful snacks with picking up fallen plums or getting paw paws out of the woods or cracking walnuts and hickory nuts. Before refrigerators even, they had homemade ice cream when the iceman came with chunks of ice for the icebox. Nothing was better than rich cream and fresh eggs in the ice cream recipe. Country kids could go to town to see a circus or to the movie show or to the skating rink. Country kids could hear music on the battery radio. They could do all the things city kids did and still know all about the country. When there was gas rationing in the 40s and WWII, country kids could sweet-talk dads to get five gallons from the elevated farm gas tanks maybe a couple times a month. And wasn't uncommon to see an old car riding the rim if there wasn't a ration stamp available for a new tire. It was best if the rim was on the side where the car could be driven off the edge of the pavement or gravel to do less damage.

City kids didn't have hills and hollers to play on, didn't have cricks to wade in, big yards to play football in or a pasture to play baseball, horses to ride, or have goats for pets. Kids in the settlement where the schools were, had to walk to school and kids in the country rode busses. Busses put to an end the advantage of the experience to have to walk miles in snow that was deeper than fence posts, as the old timers used to tell when they went to school. City kids couldn't go to the barn to see a newborn calf, or milk a cow and squirt milk to the cat. No permission cards were necessary for the Fontanet settlement kids to ride busses to the country. Country mothers and dads never knew when kids would come to stay all night but always made them feel welcome. Great friendships of the kids and these old folks were cemented for life. And the country kids stayed with the settlement kids after ballgames and not have to walk a couple miles home in the dark.

BAD LITTLE NICE GIRLS

Most country kids were nice all the time. Upon one occasion it wasn't always so. Three little girls about ages 8 and 10 were in the garden looking at the zinnies that were next to the road. There was a branch of a tree that had big leaves still on it by the road. A car was heard coming up the road and these girls decided they would throw the branch in the road as the car went by. The car was a convertible with three people in it and as it got close the tree branch was hurled. The girls thought it was funny to see the driver try to dodge it and swerved from side to side of the gravel road. Wasn't so funny when one of the passengers happened to be the big brother of one. Scared to death, all three of them, they suddenly realized they had done something very bad. The only thing that saved the little farm girl and the Kersey kids from harsh punishment was the first time blackmail probably was heard of. This brother said he wouldn't tell but his little sister had to do lots of things for him forever. For months anytime the brother wanted something, he just had to look at his little sister. If it was to go get an apple off the tree for him, his sister did it. If it was to carry a bucket of coal from the shed to the living room heater, she did it. If it was to clean the mud off his shoes, she did it. No one would believe these good girls could be so bad.. This little sister probably paid him back without his ever knowing it. After the brother and his cousin were out of school they still had crushes for two pretty girls still in school. With no telephones and a distance of seven miles between the homes, a means of communication was devised by sending notes with her on the bus. Mornings they would give her the notes with instructions to deliver them to these girls at school. She did. Evenings the high school girls would give their notes to her to take home. She did. One morning she decided to read the boys' notes and that night she read the notes the girls sent back to her brother and his cousin, Raymond. Soon she was reading the love letters out loud mornings and again on the way home. The kids laughed and so did the bus driver. Don't know that they ever found out that these mushy notes were public knowledge. She never did remember to tell her brother and cousin.

The two little neighbor Kersey girls with whom she played daily got the whooping cough. How the little girl missed her playmates! Her mother told her that she could go about a half a mile farther to play. She had to be careful when she got to the pavement and watch for cars. She was to tell Pauline's mother she could stay an hour. The little girl was so disappointed no one was home. Nearly in tears she had to walk right back home. She wanted to play so much she couldn't resist when she heard the whooping cough kids laughing as they were playing with their dolls. They were in the chicken house that she had worked hard helping sweep and clean to make it a fun place to play. It was too much to resist, so she sneaked to play with them. The kids were glad to see her too and they even breathed on each other thinking if they all had whooping cough they could play together sooner. Her naughty disobedience might never have been known if she hadn't stayed past the hour. She knew she was in trouble when she heard her mother calling "Norma, Norma Mae." Her mother was anxious so she had come to look for her and saw the little daughter coming out the driveway. She grabbed the sleeve of her dress and scolded her. She said, "If you get whooping cough I will give you a spanking each time you cough." A spanking from mom would be a smack on the leg but the tone of her voice stung and hurt more than the physical contact. The mother must have scared the whooping cough away because the little girl never got it.

Many years passed but the memories stood still. The farm girl's brother and his wife built a house on a corner of the twenty acres across the road, down a little lane and close to the Kersey's. Their son, Jim, played often with the country neighbors and they shared so much. 'Twas nothing for the back door to open and one of the kids come in to use the pencil sharpener. Many baseball games were played. How quickly 30 or 40 years went by. The brother had moved to Mattoon. When he passed away, the country neighbors came. When the sister in law passed away, four of the six neighbor "kids" came. The respect and love shown will never be forgotten. After a tear or two, there was lingering and soon stories were told. Someone asked how Jim and Susie were and learned why they could not come. Jeannie's husband Bob grinned as she recalled the time she was responsible for a ball hitting Jim in the eye. Her mother made her put on a dress, actually put on a dress, to go to the hospital the next morning to apologize. She couldn't remember if she threw the ball or batted it. But she will never forget that was one of the rare times she wore a dress. Jeannie was the one who handed the farm girl's grandson, Dane, his high school diploma. Mari C and Gladys laughed and had almost forgotten how they would play so close to dark and then be afraid to walk home. They would go to the old gnarled apple tree at the half way point and then run as fast as they could. When they got home they would yodel of a sorts so they would know all were safe. Clyde, the Indiana State Representative, and wife Karen were there with fond memories to share.

Virginia or Ginny or Aunt Gin as she was called, was a friend as well as sister in law of the 1945 junior Fontanet girl. Her brother had married Virginia April 1, 1946. When their son Jim got his first bicycle, they bought Howard's little niece her first tricycle. Linda was maybe not quite two so her granddad tied corn cobs around the pedals so she could reach them. At Virginia's funeral service one of the ministers told that often when he visited nursing homes, some would be so sad and always complaining. One such time, Virginia spoke up and said she realized she needed more care than her family could give and she came there to live. To live! And she did live at Odd Fellow-Rebekah Home seven years and was always pleasant and active in organizing groups to sing or be in a kitchen band. She befriended the other patients. Very suddenly she became quite ill and needed to be made comfortable with medication. She knew all her family and friends were with her and someone held her hand. She smiled when someone held the phone for her to hear messages from granddaughters, Robyn and Jennifer, who called from Georgia and Singapore. She loved those who visited her and made her last hours memorable.

Her favorite coat, a mink fur, hung on the door of her room. How appropriate that her daughter thought to have it put on her as she lay in the casket. Taralee, who had a degree in cosmetology, fixed her hair and polished her nails. She had been gravely ill just a few days before she quietly ceased breathing. How beautiful she looked and the sting of death was erased. How comforting to have friends and old neighbors pay respects to reflect. Her eleven year old grandson, Caleb, walked by her casket as a pall bearer. After the funeral, the 1945 junior class play character was alone in the quiet of her home and a peaceful feeling came over her. She pulled an afghan around her and remembered Ginny crocheted it for her several years ago and she had loved using it just for plain every day. She took off her earrings and smiled as she remembered that Ginny had been so proud to give them to her. They matched a beautiful necklace. Ginny had won the set playing Bingo at the nursing home and it was a prize that someone had donated. She watched out for earrings that had screw backs, which made them almost antiques and was delighted to call on the phone and say, "Norma Mae, stop in as I have something for you." During the visitation and funeral she seemed to be the one the younger ones clung to for comfort. She promised she would always be Aunt Nonie Mae to Jim and Taralee and to those nieces and nephew of Virginia: Barbara Kay, Jackie, Tammy and Tonya, Bill and his wife Judy, and cousin Paul Gene who had all called her that through many years. The farm girl was so pleased to see the neighbors she grew up with before she too, moved to Mattoon. The years of friendship had made her proud to have known them and to always keep in touch. Memories worth more than words can describe. Now she would relax and maybe even grieve for Ginny and shed the tears she had bravely held. Virginia didn't live sixty years in this world for nuthin!

TOMORROW IS HAPPY MEMORY DAY
By Norma Mae Doty Taylor

When sadness crosses our paths, it's mysteriously very sweet.
It prompts remembering challenges we've had to meet.
When often we rejoice to share thoughts with a friend,
Or ponder why sorrow seems more than we comprehend,
It's within the realm of sadness, that answers sometime come
When even in death, the memory of life is the prize that is won.

Emotions measure our expressions of feelings and growth
Treasured to share as pledged symbols of our troth.
Thoughts of joy and grief can consecrate emotions deep
Cleansing the mind and soul even as we mourn and weep.
Pain and sorrow or anything unpleasant is washed away.
Yesterday is gone, Today is here, and Tomorrow is Happy Memory Day

THIS AND THAT OF FARM LIFE

Farm kids learned how to do everything and developed character with virtues while working with mom and dad. How better to learn patience than helping a little runt pig find a nursing spot with the mama pig and learning how to be safe by having a strong board fence to reach through. And sometimes the runt had to be taken inside to be warm in a box and be fed with a bottle. Waiting for eggs to hatch also taught patience and taught kids how to mark off days on a calendar. It was fun to scribble on the eggs with a lead pencil so they could be recognized as hatching eggs. And kids didn't mess with setting hens and soon learned they were very cross while waiting to become mother hens. Watching a mother hen care for her chicks taught child rearing skills and taught kids to obey and respect their mother as the chick's responded to the cluck of the hen that was winging them in from danger or a rainstorm.

Although money was tight, there was always plenty to eat and what cash there was went for store-bought staples like flour and sugar and cocoa. Shoes for the kids and overalls and milk buckets, tin cans of pineapple and new rubber rings for the canning jars were among necessities where cash was needed.

The farm girl's father often couldn't afford a real team of horses. He had an old blind sorrel mare and borrowed a big mule from a neighbor when two horses were needed to hitch to a wagon to shuck corn or to haul sugar cane. One morning his little daughter was in the field and he made a place in the front of the wagon on a stack of sugar cane for her to sit. He would say giddup to the horses for them to go and they would stop the minute he said whoa. One afternoon when the stalks of sugar cane started rolling off the wagon, so did the little girl and she landed on the ground in front of the wagon behind the horses. Scared as he was, her dad told the horses to be steady and he picked her up to see that she was ok. He said, "Now don't tell your mom." He didn't want to lose the privilege of having these special times with his daughter or have his wife think he was careless. She would rather be outside with dad doing outdoor stuff than in the house, so she didn't tell.

She remembers how the families would take the sugar cane to her mother's Uncle Walter Cox. He had a press that squeezed the liquid from the canes. There was a horse hooked to something and the horse went around in a circle to turn a wheel. The liquid was boiled down until it was thick and brown and they called it molasses. It was used fresh and also put in jars to put on pancakes or to bake with.

As she got older, she still loved outdoorsy stuff. While some twelve-year-olds would rather be playing dolls or hopscotch, she was thrilled when asked to cultivate the corn. The sorrel blind mare had a colt and it tagged along with the team of mother and the borrowed mule. The corn was about knee high and the cultivator did two rows one side at a time. It was pretty modern because it had a seat. The shovels were on levers to raise when at the end of the row to turn around, and then the shovels were lowered. The shovels were guided with the feet the right distance from the corn plants to dig out the weeds and also pile the dirt around the roots. It was hard not to plow out the corn. Took awhile to get the knack but once learned it was a skill mastered for life. The left shovel cultivated the right side of the corn and the right shovel cultivated the left side and turned around, the process reversed itself so two times across the field plowed two rows. At the end of the row the horses stopped while the plows were lifted up and put in brackets. The horses responded to the gees or haws and the reins until they were turned around and the cultivator was positioned in the right rows. A gee command meant for the horse to turn right and the haw was left. The horses stopped while the shovels were taken off the brackets and lowered next to the corn. A giddup started them down the rows. Round and round until before you'd know it, the whole field was done. The first colt the blind mare had, was named Prince. The other one was born in June while Aunt Eva was visiting, so its name was June Eva. They grew up to be the first real team on the farm, a fine pair of horses big enough to pull a wagon of corn or a hayrack, and yet made good horses to ride.

Country kids loved to visit one another. One afternoon the Fontanet farm girl and a friend, Mary Long, decided to ride the horses. There was only one saddle and since Prince was the more spirited one, the farm girl rode him and Mary rode June Eva bareback. They headed south on the gravel road and were down the hill and around the bend when a neighbor's big old mare jumped the fence and ran towards Prince. Mary got off her horse and opened a wire gap and got inside a fenced field. Prince was turned around and headed up the road towards home. All the farm girl could think of was getting home and started yelling for her dad. She was glad she had the saddle so she could kick out at the old mare. She knew she needed to keep the mare behind her so she kept kicking with her right leg in the stirrup. The mare was short and wide with really big feet! The mare was trying to gain ground and was biting Prince. Prince was also kicking so the mare wouldn't overtake him. The farm girl was holding tight to the saddle horn and still kicking to the right. She was glad to get up the hill with only ¼ mile to go before getting to her house. She worried what she was going to do when she did get home.

She screamed loud as she could, "Dad! Dad!" She was relieved to see him come out of the front yard to the road. He had never heard such clatter of eight hoofs pounding the gravel. When he realized what was happening, he yelled for her to keep coming and when she got closer, he told her to pull Prince sharply to the left. The mare was clumsy and nearly fell trying to stop so abruptly. The dad picked up a tree limb and hit the mare hard enough to slow her down and stun it. He then talked sternly to settle the mare down. The dad told his daughter to quickly take Prince to the barn and lock him in.

That was quite a fete for these young riders to escape what could have been a very serious disaster. Lucky the farm girl was a good rider and too bad a movie camera crew wasn't there. Would have been no need to have a professional stunt rider!

Riding was fun and the farm girl liked working in fields even before Prince and June Eva. She loved hay time. The iron rake was a one-horse pulled one. She rode the rake and used the foot pedal. Without the pedal being pushed down, the hay tines collected the hay. When the foot pushed the pedal down, the half circle tines raised to dump the hay in a row or it might have been the other way around. It was so long ago, it might have been a lever. When the field was raked the baler could go down the rows or her dad could pick it up with a pitchfork and toss it on a hay wagon to take to the barn. What wouldn't fit in the barn was made into big haystacks. They were fun to slide down on. Better to be outside rakin than inside bakin!

Balers cost a lot of money so there was only one that served a large area. He would make appointments so the farmers could cut their hay in time to have it dry in the fields at least 3 days. The custom baler charged a set price for each bale. He would either bring a crew to pick up the bales from the field in a wagon to be hauled to the barn for storage or the farmer would have his own wagon and kids or hired hands. Farmers watched the signs and listened to the radio hoping to cut when it wasn't going to be raining. The first cuttings of alfalfa was around Decoration Day, the second July 4 and Labor Day was the third cutting which was the premier cutting. Cows liked the first cutting with its course stems, and horses the second and sheep much preferred the third with more delicate stems and leaves. There was also timothy hay that horses liked that the farmers raised and raked and sometimes clover.

At the milk barn, lots of current events were discussed from what was read in the newspaper or heard on the radio. Or maybe an issue could be discussed so that the kids got a lesson from hearing about how someone else got in trouble by doing something or not doing something. Lessons like this were never forgotten. It was also a time of sharing neighborhood or countryside happenings when someone turned a car over on the gravel road while not driving careful, or how Mr. so and so got in the wrong house after too much to drink.

Mrs. Miller's husband had been asked by a neighbor to help with a sick cow. It got late and she went to bed leaving the coal oil lamp lit. Pretty soon she felt the soft mattress on the bed tip and she asked how the cow was. No one answered and she asked again, "How is Kessel's cow?" and didn't understand the mumbled answer. She turned over and found it was not her husband but a neighbor man. About that time Mr. Miller came home. The husband soon got the bewildered sleepy man out of the bed, out of the house and pointed him to his own house another mile away. Next day there was a long talk and it was thought Mr. Miller emphasized enough points that shed a lot of light on the subject of consequences of drinking liquor that might have impressed the neighbor to make more efforts to stay sober. Being discussed while milking cows, the kids got the message and agreed with their mother's philosophy of prohibition.

Any opportunity that came up was one used to learn about Creation. The farm girl's dad believed the story in the Bible that God created the earth and made man in His own image. He often quoted from the Bible and pointed out all the wonders of nature. He saw the beauty of trees, the amazing sunsets, the cycles of the growing seasons, the rain and the sunshine. He talked about how God made the world and made man. He made the story simple that God made the first man and woman and everyone that was born after that was a Creation of God. There was a theory, called Darwin's Theory that was taught in school. The school principal was a brilliant man and a wonderful teacher. One day in a high school class he was teaching this theory that man evolutioned from an ape. The Darwin Theory said that man came from monkeys. Everyone was listening and there wasn't much interest or response shown by the class. The principal called on one student by name and asked her how she felt about the theory of Evolution. Didn't take the farm girl long to reply, "Well, you might not know whether, or you might believe you came from a monkey, but thank God I know I didn't!

Many years later this student wrote a letter to him and mentioned that he had been the best teacher possible. He had a flare for mathematics and when he recognized a student had an aptitude for math, he would often make time to teach beyond the usual algebra and geometry which was all that was ordinarily offered in most township high schools. He had flash cards for highschoolers and they memorized squares of numbers that came in handy long after graduation. Learning that 10 x 10 was 100, 11 x 11 was 121, 12 x 12 was 144, 13 x 13 was 169, 14 x 14 was 196, for examples, made for quick answers to estimate cost or size of something. People thought his students were extra smart to get answers so quick without a pencil and paper. And everyone in Fontanet knew the multiplication tables by heart front and back since 3rd grade. She thanked him for being the administrator of the school and for his dedication to the students.

She expressed her hope that through the years, if he didn't already, he had come to believe the Bible account of Creation and not the theory of Evolution. She wrote that she remembered him and other teachers for whom she would always be grateful.

Another admired teacher who didn't live sixty years in this world for nuthin!

DEPENDABILITY LEARNED ON THE FARM

Dependability was not to be escaped or taken lightly and instilled characteristics that lasted for life. Kids knew that the cows had to come to the barn for milking at night at a certain time. Most of the time they came on their own, but if you needed to go someplace early, the cows had to be brought out of the pastures. Cows had bells but late afternoons were times for cows to hide in thickets or groves of sassafras and they were quiet as mice so there was never a tiny tinkle from their bells. And they would never lay in the same place. Kids were lucky if they found them in the first places they looked. When the cows were found they were never in a hurry to line up in the lane to the barn. Once the cows reached the barn lot, no one wanted to forget to close the lane with the wire gap so they wouldn't get out and go back to the pasture. Usually her dad and her brother did the milking. Sometimes the little farm girl would help her brother to surprise dad. When their dad worked in the coal mine and he would come home tired, the kids were thrilled to tell him the cows were milked! That is how kids were, they got their kicks out of helping out. No kid ever thought about not being dependable to make sure the cows were up from the pasture on time. Fresh hay and grain were put in the stanchion stalls for the cows to eat while they were being milked. Most people had large fenced areas around the barn and cows were kept in the barn lot overnight.

Her brother had a paper route. He will be remembered as the Fontanet Cowboy who could toss the newspapers right on target as he rode a white star faced almost black horse at a gallop. It was dangerous for his customers to have a rain barrel and sometimes accidentally or otherwise, the Terre Haute Tribune had to be dried out in the oven or over the clothesline before it could be read. It has been said that boys only aggravated girls they liked. He must have liked 'em all and he would grin to himself if he saw girls walking along the road, especially after a rain. He delighted in scolding Beauty for not getting over as the girls would jump out of the way after being splashed from a mud puddle. He gave his little sister an allowance of ten cents a week. One week he needed to keep more money for himself and gave his sister a big nickel and told her it was more than a little dime.

The county fair was a highlight event for the year. Horse shows, exhibits, carnivals and lots of cotton candy and goodies not got at home. One year the horses were taken from the farm to go to the fair and be in the parade. One was a horse named Beauty and she was well trained. Her rider could go from the saddle under the belly and back in the saddle while the horse was running. He could rope the fastest calf. He could be on the horse and have the horse put all four feet on a block about 36 inches square. He seldom used the stirrups to mount but would run and put his hands on the horse's rump and swing himself forward to the saddle. The other was a big pony named Dolly. The horses were just right for a 16 year old and a 6 year old brother and sister. Riding in the parade was fun and having a grandstand of people watch made the event one never to forget. After the parade and most of the crowd had left, Beauty was taken out on the track and put through some of her tricks just for fun. He had Beauty bucking while he held onto the saddle horn with one hand and had her jumping hurdles. Riding Beauty off to the side, he got off and put his little sister on the tall graceful, black horse with a white star on her forehead. Her hoofs were wrapped with white cloths to add to her regal appearance. From the grandstands a woman yelled, "Take that baby off that bucking horse; that beast will kill that little girl." Beauty plodded off like a plow horse because this little girl had ridden her many times before. Beauty knew when and when not to do her tricks or bucking and she knew who was riding her. Beauty and Dolly were put in the trailer for the 15 miles back to the farm for a drink of water from the branch and fresh timothy hay in the barn. They would be glad to have a big pasture to run and play.

MORE THAN JUST A BARN..
written by Norma Doty Taylor

..............If I were an artist or a poet
I'd paint a picture and before you'd know it,
There it would be on canvas -- a barn
and a story about life on an Indiana farm.

Probably built in 1920, before I came along,
animals were cozy in the barn, 30-ft wide 40 long,
one side for the horses, the other for cows,
pigs on the end, with feedway below the haymow.

During a blizzard, dad shoveled a path to the barn;
how excited he was that twin calves had been born.
Those rare twins I wanted to see, but I had the mumps.
Dad bundled me, snuck me out and said, "Don't tell yer mum!"

The Terre Haute Tribune was delivered by my brother,
as he rode his horse Beauty thru Fontanet hills and hollers.
He taught her tricks; could make her buck like a charm;
rewarded her with hay and sweet strawed stall in the barn.

Many years have passed; we don't live there any more.
I'd love to visit the barn and do just one more chore.
I hope my brother Howard and Beauty are riding golden streets,
as mom and dad are planting flowers for angels to see.

And as for me, if my Heavenly mansion is half as nice
as I remember that old barn, even with its mice,
I'll be there with values I learned on that little farm!
If I could, I'd share a poem with you...about the barn...

CHRISTMAS WITH GRANDMA AND GRANDPA COX

The founders of the Fontanet United Brethren church lived back through the woods, across a crick and up a hill from their daughter, Alice, and her family. Christmas morning of 1935 they were looking forward to the daughter's family coming for dinner. No doubt pumpkin pies were baked, the old hen had been boiled and the dumplings ready to drop in the broth. It started snowing early with snowflakes big as saucers, really clusters big as saucers and within half an hour quite an accumulation had covered the ground and was making big drifts. Grandpa cut a limb from an oak tree that instead of losing its leaves in fall, kept its leaves but they turned brown. He was carrying a tradition from years back. No one remembers what it symbolized or that the tree limb had decorations.

At the daughter's house kids were woke up with their dad and his French harp playing Christmas songs, the favorite being Silent Night and then a rousing Jingle Bells. It was probably the only morning of the year they got out of bed before 5:15. The Christmas tree was a cedar branch from the old tree in the front yard and was festive with strings of popcorn and red cranberries. After Christmas the birds would have a feast. About every day for a week there were wrapped presents put under the tree for the grownups leaving plenty of space for Santa to put gifts for the under ten year olds. With the snow coming down so hard it soon become apparent that they couldn't go to grandma's and how sad and disappointing that was.

All of a sudden there was a stomping sound and big knocks on the back door and someone all covered with snow came in the kitchen. It was a cousin that had been staying with grandpa and grandma. "How in the world did you get here in all this snow?" He said it wasn't easy but he thought he could figure out a way for everyone to still go to the scrumptious Christmas dinner. He thought the seven-year old could ride the horse with her brother and if they went thru the bottoms, they could make it. And the cousin was young, big and tall and thought he and the dad could help the mom. The plan worked and the horse almost had to swim the snow because the drifts were up to its belly. And the tall strong young man and the dad helped the petite mom. A Christmas never to forget.

CHRISTMAS ON THE OLE HOMEPLACE

Christmases on the farm were always ones to remember.

The first Christmas the son was home after being gone four years overseas was very special and another not to be forgotten. Presents under the tree were supposed to be secret and no one usually even attempted to feel or shake until at least Christmas Eve. The dad was amused as he saw his son on hands and knees feeling and shaking packages with his name on them. One was probably easy to detect except its color because it was a brimmed hat that was only wrapped in red tissue. Being caught, the son grinned and said he had looked forward to this Christmas at home more than any other before. This was the same Christmas when the daughter was 18 years old. Her dad had seen a big brown Teddy bear in the window of Kresge's in Terre Haute. He just knew this would be the perfect gift for daddy's girl.. The bear in the window was the last one and the store manager couldn't take it out of the window until the morning of Christmas Eve and he promised to save it. Christmas Eve morning was snowing and the roads were slick but that didn't keep the dad from driving the 15 miles from the farm to Terre Haute to get the bear! When he was handed the teddy bear, the Christmas Spirit really hit him! He took time to browse and take advantage of many marked down prices. The old Chevy looked like Santa's sleigh as it slid on the snow-packed roads back to the farmhouse where soon the gifts would be put under the Christmas tree.

Another Christmas Eve it had been snowing and was like a blizzard. The mom just knew their son and his wife and their first grandson, Jimmy, would not be able to make it from Mattoon to the farm. Even though it was long past the expected arrival time, the Dad just kept saying, "They'll be here pretty soon," Sure enough the car lights were blurred with heavy snow but could be seen as the car turned in the yard enough to be safe off the road. Jimmy's aunt barely made it home after being out on a date. It was getting late and everyone needed to be in bed, especially three year old little boys on Christmas Eve. His aunt told her nephew that she had seen Santa about five miles away and she thought Jimmy would jump right in bed. Instead his big brown eyes got wider and wider and he was determined to stay up to see Santa. Because of the failed psychology, his mother made this aunt Nonie Mae stay up and rock him, and rock him, and rock him well into the Christmas morning wee hours. Jimbo, as he was affectionately sometimes called, was lucky that Santa didn't get tired of waiting for him to go to sleep.

The dad passed away in January of 1956 and after a few months, the mother was so sentimental that she didn't think she could stay on the farm. She rented an apartment in Terre Haute. She would tell people, "On South 6th Street. Do you know where the Garden Apartments are? People would remember that they were new and quite expensive. She would then say, "My apartment is in the old house across the street." The next Christmas time, she bought a small artificial tree and some new decorations She fixed food for the Christmas dinner and, of course, had gifts for the family. Christmas Eve the phone rang and it was her son, Howard. "Mom, me and Ginny are out here at the farm. I have put wood and coal in the furnace and the house is nice and warm. We put up a tree and have your decorations on it. We found the cardboard angels and the Santa Claus and have them hanging from the ceiling. And we have a hen ready to bake in the morning. We will have Christmas as usual on the farm." His mother was touched with excitement as she gathered the brightly wrapped robes and house slippers, socks and shirts and books and color crayons and embroidered pillowcases. She felt like Santa Claus as she asked the elves to help carry stuff into the farm house. Her son said the only time he ever wanted not to have Christmas on the home place farm, was when he was overseas and had no other choice. The house was warm and festive. She missed her husband and the son and daughter missed their dad, and the kids missed granddad. If you were very quiet, you could almost hear the dad playing on the French harp as he did so many years every Christmas morning, Silent Night and Jingle Bells. Christmas on the farm was beautiful and soon the mother moved back home to the house she really did love.

She maintained the home place so much enjoyed by her son and daughter and their families. A place to go home! The same Christmas celebrations were enjoyed for many years with the cardboard angels and Santa hanging from the ceiling. She decided to get an artificial tree which was more convenient for her but it looked almost real with the old familiar ornaments. Two little great grandchildren were welcomed and 1979 was their first Christmas spent on the farm. Probably in about 1950 their great grandfather, Grover, had made a cradle from split hickory small limbs. It was placed under the tree with a doll to represent the Baby Jesus. In 1979 the doll was taken out of the cradle for awhile. A great grandson, Dane Matthew Devereaux, was born Nov 24 and how proud this little baby would have made his great grandfather. He was laid in the cradle and a treasured picture was taken with the 616 Kodak. A great granddaughter, Hollie Niccole Taylor, was born August 20, 1979 and spent her first Christmas on the farm at the family traditional gathering. They made a lapful for great grandmother. Too young to remember,

Sixty Years in This Wicked World for Nuthin

they won't be let forget as they are told the stories about grandparents and greats. Those who remembered when Christmas mornings were traditionally being awakened with the Dad playing on the French harp Jingle Bells and Silent Night and sometimes he would have to go to the barn to bring in some hidden presents. And no one knew in 1979 that only one more Christmas would be happy in the house on the little farm that no one had lived in except this Doty family. Two other great granddaughters, Sheena Jane and Bridget Jean Taylor missed Christmases on the farm and they will be told stories to let them know how much they would have been loved and are loved because of the dedication and sincerity of their hardy ancestors. A great great grandson, Caleb, will be told stories about the farm where his grandfather, Howard Doty, grew up and rode horses and flew an airplane and made a landing strip at the end of the 20 acres plot across the road from the farm house. These offspring will know from where they come and who were the ones who helped determine their features and traits. A heritage of which they will be proud.

MANY 75 MILE TRIPS

There were thousands of miles driven between Mattoon and Fontanet and if everyone had a nickel for each mile they drove they would be quite wealthy. Grandchildren loved going to the farm. When just Grandma Doty lived there, they saw pictures and heard stories about how it was when Grandpa was there so they felt they knew him too. The Grandma loved having visits from the grandsons and she preferred them one at a time. She could spend undivided time with one and she read to them until they could read to her. She was careful that they pronounced the words just right and then she would ask them questions about what they had read. When the family would visit the homeplace, the farm girl's mother would come bustling out the back enclosed porch door. She was probably waiting by the window looking up the road so she wouldn't miss them. The two little grandsons would hurry ahead to see her first. Steve the youngest would get to her first and hug her and get his hugs and kisses. The older one, Tracy, always hung back just looking at her until she would reach for him and then they would hug. One time Steve was first to get his greeting and Tracy still hung back. Steve pushed him towards his Granny and said, "Go on and hug her.." Two little boys each in their way so different. And what they liked to eat was different. One liked candy and sweets but wouldn't touch the fruits his brother liked. As they would grow older more memories accumulated of being taken to Sunday School and church in Fontanet, of helping in the garden and stringing the beans to be cooked with chunks of jowl bacon. Granny loved to read to them and listen to them read, played a board game with them that their grandfather had made. They called it the Crazy Game It was homemade before the game of Concentration came out.

Many miles were added on trips driven to the Bean Dinner, trips to family reunions or about any excuse to get to see one another. There were trips bringing mom to visit or taking grandkids to visit grandmother. On one of these trips while looking on a top shelf of a shed on the farm, some old fruit jars were found. They had raised embossed letters that said Mason's Patented November 30th 1858. The mom said they were brought from her parents' old homeplace and the daughter could have them. These jars started a whole collection of old fruit jars that remind the daughter of her heritage when these old jars were used to can foods necessary for surviving the winters until new vegetables and fruits would be in season.

The farm girl's mother's sister, Eva, lived in Mattoon and it was a good place to visit and get acquainted with her neighbors. Guess that is how both the mom's kids ended up married and living in Mattoon. It was so much fun having the phone ring and the brother would say, "Hey, how did mom fix those tomatoes we used to put over mashed potatoes?" She spected he soon had some cooking on the stove by making a cream sauce of butter and flour and adding half and half cream before adding a can of tomatoes simmering to near boil until they were thickened. Grandma had showed their mother how and they were made with home-canned tomatoes rather than store bought. The brother's wife Ginny was a good cook but he wouldn't trust her with old family recipes. She didn't care and always was glad to have him cook. He made good goulash and never the same way but it always ended up delicious. Wonder if he taught his little daughter, Taralee, any family cooking secrets? There was nothing that this brother and sister wouldn't do for one another. Probably because the sister never told him how she read the mushy letters on the bus that he and a girl in school wrote to each other and he had forgiven her for throwing the tree limb on the car that nearly wrecked the car that he was riding in.

The brother wasn't much of a walker. He was a handsome little boy in a picture on his first vehicle which was a big thin-tired tricycle. In another picture he was in a little cart hitched to a goat. As he grew older on the farm he had horses to ride or could drive his dad's old Auburn or Chevys. When he went in the army he drove a truck in the quartermaster division, seems like it was the 38th. After his discharge of four years in the army, he drove for his own Black and White Cab Company in Mattoon. Later he drove semi trucks for McBrides and Hayes Freight from Mattoon to St Louis and worked for Eastern Express from Terre Haute to the east coast until he retired. He learned to fly in his little two-seater Luscome and had a runway on the farm in Indiana.

While on vacation one time, he helped his sister's husband on a project making a road that also made a dam for a nice pond of water. There was a big hill down and a big hill up that had to be walked several times a day. At the beginning of the project he huffed and puffed but by the end of the week, he was almost running up and down the hills like a pro runner. He had done more walking that week than in his lifetime. The hard work was worth it when later he bought a boat to put on the pond for many hours of pleasure. It was very special doing things together with these two families of a brother and sister. The nephews loved having their uncle spend time with them. He talked about having goats when he was a little boy back on the farm in Indiana He talked so much in fact that his nephew decided he wanted goats. The nannies were fun and easy to handle but the billy was another story. When it would jump its pen no one could handle it until the nephew would get home from school. It seemed about every time the brother went to visit his sister, he'd see a funny grin and he knew the billy was lose and he was expected to catch it and tie it up til he could find where the goat got out and fix the fence. He was the best brother and uncle anyone ever had.

Howard was a loving father and his sister wrote a poem for his daughter

Norma Mae Doty Taylor

To Taralee Doty by her Aunt Nonie Mae

Was an eventful Special Day
On July 24, 1964
A precious baby was born, and say
Who could ask for more?

Now seems like yesterday
But, alas, it's 25 years
1989 and a Special Birthday
Reminisce the smiles and tears.

"You've come along way, baby.."
So proud you ought to be
Let me assure you, not maybe
Admired by all, especially me!

Grandmothers Heath and Doty, the very best
Adored you, their legacy left.
Loved by nieces, cousins and brother
Aunts, uncles, mom and dad
Like no other.

You've earned degrees, studied much
Talents unfolded like buds on trees
Happy Birthday and lots of luck
You're an honor to our name.. Taralee

Sixty Years in This Wicked World for Nuthin

It was the hardest thing his sister had to endure seeing her brother become ill and pass away. Nephews and nieces knew how much they would miss him. Tracy and Steve were honored to be pall bearers. Cousins who lived within 500 miles came to visitation or the funeral. Retired truck drivers sent flowers from several states. Neighbors who still lived near the Fontanet farm came.

This brother had a passion for driving. In his retirement he loved working for local car dealers. When a dealer needed a driver to make an exchange, Howard was given a call. If the local dealer had sold a red car but only had a blue one on the lot, exchanges were made between dealers. Often he would drive within a three hundred radius and always loved comparing the many new models he drove. A local doctor would often order his new car from the factory and didn't want it loaded on a car carrier so he would pay Howard to go to Detroit to drive it to Mattoon.

When one of these car dealers learned of his death, he immediately offered the family the use of a car. The family felt honored for the use of the finest Cadillac as they followed the hearse to Dodge Grove Cemetery in Mattoon. His sister remembered the story her dad had told about how her brother when the age of 4 had tugged on his father's pant leg to inquire about a man who was different. She remembered how her father had simply explained that the man was a good friend. She thought to herself that the Cadillac dealer was the same as the man those 65 years ago that was different. She thought too, that Mr. Rutledge would chuckle at the story same as the man did 65 years ago when Howard saw his first man of color. Her brother was a friend of all.

No one was ever loved more! This brother didn't live sixty years in this world for nuthin.

A WIDOWED MOTHER ON THE FARM

The farm girl's mother loved her house on the farm and was glad she only lived a short time in an apartment.. That was the time after her beloved husband had passed away and she was lonely and being in the house without him was more than she thought she could bear. She was glad her son insisted they have that next Christmas as usual on the farm.. She never forgot the agony of how close they had come to losing it when times were bad and they went through the foreclosure and buying it back. Progress included electricity coming to the rural area which enabled a pump system to pipe water from a spring-fed well to the house, changing a big walk-in pantry to a bathroom, and putting the wood icebox out on the back porch to become an antique. How proud the farm girl's dad would be that her mother had stayed on the farm and continued to make it a home for their family to visit.

The farm girl coveted the recipes she had of her mother's good cooking. Many favorites but especially no one made cream pies like her mother. She kept the recipe in a safe place so she wouldn't lose it.

CREAM PIE
½ cup sugar
4 tablespoons flour
¼ teaspoon salt
2 cups milk
2 egg yolks, slightly beaten
2 tablespoons table fat
1 teaspoon vanilla
9-inch baked pastry shell

Mix dry ingredients with a little of the milk. Add rest of milk. Cook over boiling water, stirring until thick. Cover and cook 15 minutes longer. Add table fat and vanilla. Pour filling into baked shell, cool slightly, and cover with meringue. Bake at 320 degrees (slow oven) 12 to 15 minutes or at 425 degrees (hot oven) 4 to 5 minutes. She wonders whatever happened to the aluminum double boiler her mother used for these wonderful pie fillings.

Her mother made variations for cream pie – Slice 2 bananas into the pie shell before adding the filling. Coconut cream pie – add 1/3 cup shredded coconut to cream filling; turn into a baked pie shell. Top with meringue and sprinkle with coconut. For heavenly chocolate cream pie – Make filling as for cream pie, adding ½ cup milk, ¼ cup sugar, and 2 ½ squares chocolate. .

The Meringue recipe was 2 egg whites, ¼ teaspoon salt and 4 tablespoons sugar. She beat the egg whites with salt until stiff. And then beat in the sugar slowly until smooth and glossy. Sometimes she would whip the country fresh Jersey cream instead of meringue.

Her mother made potato salad that was the envy of the neighborhood. And probably because she cooked everything with rich cream and homemade butter.

COOKED SALAD DRESSING
3 tablespoons vinegar
1 egg or 2 egg yolks, beaten
1/3 cup milk
1 tablespoon table fat
½ teaspoon salt
1/3 teaspoon sugar
12 teaspoon dry mustard
Paprika and celery seed if desired.

Add vinegar to egg and beat. Stir in rest of ingredients Cook over boiling water; stir constantly until thickened. Makes about ¾ cup.

Her mother's many friends and neighbors found pleasure in asking to take her to church or to town. She loved the Church of God and the Fontanet United Brethren Church, where she was a charter member, and whichever friend offered a ride, that is where she attended services. At various times she would have a gift for her drivers and would pay for lunch when they took her to town. Her mother's brother lived 1/8 mile away and they had many rides together to town and reminisced about the years growing up and she often went with him to churches where he was a lay minister.

The Bean Dinner was still a highlight but she often mentioned that not many of her friends were living to attend. At the Bean Dinner in 1981 she was glad to see her good old friend, Mrs. Inglert, and they talked and talked about how their families were. It started to mist rain and the grown farm girl held her mom's arm as they hurried to the car. Her mother was a little short of breath but they made it to the car before getting too wet. Her mother wasn't feeling her usual best and could only work an hour at a time in her garden, and had to rest while doing her housecleaning chores. She just couldn't understand why she got tired. It was planned for the mother to go home with her daughter who lived in the country from Mattoon. As she finished putting clothes in her suitcase, she took a second look all around her house. She drank in the flowered wallpaper she loved in the big dining room and living room combined. The red drapes and the snow-white sheers reflected her taste in decorating. She probably remembered it had been sixty years since they had the house built and she had lived twenty five years alone after her husband died. As they drove by Mrs. Kersey's, she remarked how they had been like sisters the many years they were closest neighbors, by Beshaw's store that had been so convenient, on through Terre Haute to Mattoon. She had been to Mattoon many times and as she got older, her children thought she might stay longer but she always found reasons she had to get back to the farm. This time she seemed more serious and made an endearing comment as she passed familiar places and homes of her many friends. She might have felt relief that the curtains on the enclosed back porch had been washed, starched and ironed just last month so maybe she need not hurry home with that as the excuse. She felt confident that her neighbor would take good care of Sparky, her beloved Dalmatian. She was glad she had canned the last of the beets and the garden had been mowed by her granddaughter's husband, Johnnie. Johnnie's father was a Fontanet High School student that was in the 1928 agriculture class that Orville Redenbacher took to her parent's orchard. The student didn't know then that his son would marry the orchard owner's great granddaughter. A chain of events with years of memories.

During the hour or so drive, the mother and daughter talked some but were mostly silent with thoughts about leaving the farm house soon to be in Mattoon where mom could spend time with both her children. Mornings the mother would get up and be dropped off in town while her daughter went to her job at the Curtis Mathes television store. The mom loved her son's wife's mother, who lived with them, and they were the same age. Mrs. Heath was a wonderful cook and lunches were gourmet. One morning mom felt tired and not like riding to town. Later in the day her son in law noticed she needed to be in the hospital. She was experiencing some pain. The nurses soon had her comfortable. During the month she was there, she would be heard whispering, "Dear Jesus, help me." For her birthday the nurses made a poster that they signed and hung on the wall at the foot of her bed.. One morning a nurse asked the daughter. "Does your mother really live on a farm in Indiana?" Proudly the daughter replied, "Yes, yes indeed! She lives on a farm in the house she and my daddy had built in the early 1920's."

On her birthday, October 22, 1981, the mother felt like taking a walk in the hall assisted by her daughter. They walked to a hospital waiting room by the elevator and exchanged some nods and smiles. She announced proudly with extra strength in her voice, "Today is my birthday, my 89th one!" She twisted her petite hips to the right and a sway to the left and then to the right again, just as cute as a button celebrating her birthday before she quietly passed away November 5. 1981.

Her son and daughter made funeral arrangements to celebrate her life. It would be in Terre Haute at Thomas Funeral home where many of the family had been before. They chose a soft pink silky robe with a green edging on the collar and the brother and sister were drawn to the casket with its soft green satin lining. They could picture their beautiful mother as she would be shown for visitation. The car list for the procession to North Terre Haute Rose Lawn Cemetery included nearest of kin, relatives and many friends. The sad day had its humor. No one figured out how grown grandson, Jim, nearly got left at the cemetery. He was talking with old neighbor friends and when he realized his family had gone, he got a ride with friends back to the funeral home where his car was. Life wouldn't be worth living without humor. Mrs. Heath was so sad that her son in law's mother had passed away and she said it was the most inspirational and beautiful funeral service she had been to. No one knew twenty days later as she would be making Thanksgiving date pudding, that she would suddenly slump over for the last breath of her beautiful 88 years. How joyous it must be when Heaven's gate opens and moms and dads, brothers and sisters, friends, children, grandchildren, aunts and uncles, cousins, and neighbors can see their loved ones walking up the golden stairs!

A WEDDING AND ESTABLISHED HOME

It must have been an intended term of fate who would be farmers and who would not.

In 1915 after dating for four years, a 24 year and 22 year became husband and wife. They later would be the farm girl's mother and dad. The bride walked a mile and half to Fontanet to catch the train to Terre Haute where she met her groom.

The newlyweds, Grover and Alice Doty, returned to Burnett on the train where they had set up their home. They had saved a hundred dollars to furnish three rooms. An ornate iron bed and oak dresser with a tilt mirror followed them wherever they moved. The kitchen table was a prized possession that had been handed down from his father when the mother died and his parents' home was broken. In a couple years the newlyweds needed a larger house which took them to Spelterville nearer to Terre Haute where a son was born.

The wife especially missed her country roots. It didn't take much persuasion for them to decide to take their 3-year old son and find some acreage where they could live on a farm. They found 40 acres with a rural Brazil Indiana address. It was within walking distance of a little town called Fontanet about a mile and half away. The price wasn't cheap and they were actually advised that it was too much to pay. The father had some experience with gardening and thought he was great material to be a farmer. He had saved enough from his job as a railroad telegraph operator to make a down payment and also have enough to build a new house. Again he was warned that spending cash for a new house was not smart on ground with a mortgage. He had a contractor help build the house from plans the couple had drawn.

It featured the south side as being the dining and living room combined which made it about thirty feet long by about fifteen feet wide. There was a big round oak table that was inviting and could always make room for one more. The big room was a gathering place for relatives and neighbors to visit and have parties. For many years there was a neighborhood get together about once a month. Sometimes there would be a theme and always lots of carry in food and games were played. There was a golden oak pump organ and sometimes there was a lot of singin'. The organ was an 1895 Story and Clark and stood almost to the eight and a half foot ceiling. The organ had a half circle beveled mirror and doors and beautiful carved spools at the top. The farm mom could play by ear, tunes like "Turkey in the Straw" and "She'll Be Coming Round the Mountain" or "When the Saints Go Marchin In." The dad and daughter were almost mad at the mom for selling the organ to a nephew, Hurley Green. She wanted a piano. She told Hurley that if he ever didn't want the organ, to please sell it back. Several years later Hurley and his wife, Frieda, moved and didn't have room for the organ and he sold it back for the same $5. Today the farm girl has it as a treasured heirloom and she wouldn't take a million for it!

Kids played games around the round oak dining room table and continued when they were teenagers. Rummy was a favorite card game. Hard fast rules were laid out. There would be no grumbling or arguing or cheating. One snowy afternoon teen cousins and neighbors were having fun until two or three argued that the other had picked up two cards instead of one and voices were raised and not so nice words were used. The father of the house did not say a word. He just took a card and scooped the rummy spreads up with the rest of the deck and opened the heating stove door and threw the cards in. The kids couldn't continue the game with only cards they had in their hands. They learned this dad was a man of his word. His rules were good and they had been bad. A week later a new deck of cards was found on the table and many more games were played but no one ever forgot the rules again.

On another cold afternoon, the mom and dad were playing rummy with their 10-year-old. The little girl was not having very good luck and she was losing the game. When it was time to bring some wood from the porch for the heating stove, they asked her to go get it. When she came back the cards had been dealt and when she picked hers up she had some really good cards that would score for her. How happy she was and it pleased the parents that they had picked out some special cards for her so she could make her score higher and maybe even win the game.

To start his country venture the new farmer borrowed a team from a brother in law and some equipment from his father in law and the first crops were good. He worked in the coal mine during winters. He added a barn and bought some milk cows and a couple pigs to be brood sows. A chicken house soon housed the baby chicks hatched in the kerosene-heated incubator that was in one end of the dining room. This young farmer had worked with his dad and learned some skills of carpentry. Just a respectable distance from the house he built the building for toilet facilities, called by some to be the outhouse. These outhouses were also hideouts from the world to browse last year's Sears and Roebuck catalog or to muse over a problem, and great to skirt off to when it was time to do dishes. And 'twasn't unsual to be accompanied by a pal, or mother and daughter, cousin or friend. Lots of confidential matters were solved there. The new facility was built so one did not have to wait on the other but could sit together on a two-holer.

The door to door salesmen were always welcome and sometimes you got well acquainted. If they knew you needed something, they would always help. One time the cows had squeezed through a gate and were about to run down the road just as the kid selling Grit came by. He sure was handy to run and head the cows back to the barn lot and even fixed the gatepost so they couldn't get out again.

Milk and eggs were sold to the people in Fontanet. There was a huckster truck that came weekly who also bought eggs. On huckster days the farm wife had her eggs washed clean and often traded them for fresh fish and hoped she would get some cash too. What a treat for supper – fish with fried potatoes and cornbread.

The McNess man had big suitcases of liniments and salves, extracts and spices, and cans of pudding mixes. He always came before the last of the big bottle of vanilla was used. He could diagnose any ache or pain and prescribe the right liniment.

There was the Fuller Brush man, the Rawleigh man, the Stanley Home Products lady, the kids selling the Grit magazine, the Prairie Farmer man who sold the magazine and gave you a tin painted sign that the property was protected by the Prairie Farmer, and trucks with watermelons, besides the grocery huckster truck.

One afternoon several women gathered to have a Stanley Party. Kids too young to be in school, got to go and they had to be still while the Stanley lady talked about brooms and mops and degreaser and germtrol. There was snow on the ground and too cold to play outside. They got the fidgets, but stifled their giggles, and could hardly wait for the refreshments of hot sassafras tea and oatmeal raisin cookies. Nearly all the Ladies Aid women came and some stayed after the party to catch up on any news they might have missed since the last quilting.

One evening the Prudential Insurance man stopped by to collect the three month-policy fees. He noticed the little girl was leaning her head in a pillow on the old leather duofold. She usually was bubbling over with excitement when he came and shared the news of what she had been doing. Asked what was wrong, he was told that she had an earache. The insurance man knew they didn't have a car and he said if they could call the doctor and if he would come to the office, he would take the little girl and her mother to Terre Haute. The nearest telephone in the neighborhood was down the road and back a lane about a three quarter mile. The little girl's brother jumped on his horse, Beauty, and soon was back with news that the doctor had been contacted and they could meet him in the office in an hour. The ear condition was serious and the ear eye and nose specialist, Dr. Allen, used a syringe with a warm liquid and said if she wasn't better by the next day, to come back and he would operate for mastoid. She slept all night and never had those bad old earaches again. Hucksters, door to door salesmen, doctors and Prudential Insurance men didn't live sixty years in this world for nuthin.

HOT SUMMER DAYS AND NIGHTS

On one of the hottest nights in July if there would be a breeze it would be from the south or west. Wasn't unusual for everyone to take a pillow and sleep on the floor by the south window and west door. One such night the farm girl's dad heard someone stop a car outside and walk up the path to the house and rattle the screen door. He could smell alcohol and loudly said, "Hey, who are you and what do you want?" The man asked how did he get to Chicago. Well Chicago was about 200 miles away and not thought of much down there on the farm. Her dad was quick to say, "Just as fast as you can, you get back in your car and keep going the direction you are going until you find Chicago." The man said, "Gee, thanks a lot" and staggered back out to his car and was never heard of again by those who were sleeping on the floor that July night. The farm girl's daddy did reach up to see if the screen door was latched. It wasn't so he latched it. He also said, "Listen, can you hear the green stalks of corn growin in the field.... This hot weather sure is making us a good crop."

It seemed like the hottest day of the year when the Sunday School picnic would be. One year it was decided instead of women fixing picnic baskets, that it would be held at Brazil in the park. There was a concession park with hot dogs and other treats. The farm girl's dad always had a keen eye for kids with no or not much money. He always made sure they had a sandwich and potato chips. There was a tub of cold drinks and when it was time to go home, the Sunday School paid for ice cream bars for everyone. The women sat on benches and talked, and the men pitched horseshoes while the kids played on the slides and swings.

LIVIN' ON FARM CLOSE TO GRANDMA

Moving to the country also put a couple and their family close to relatives. They could go around a square on roads to get to grandma and grandpa's house. Their house and farm was back off the road about a half mile or they could walk straight back thru a field, cross a little crick, and up some hills to get there. Kids could walk over the hills and a field to visit and they always knew they would be welcome. It was not as far as going on the road and much safer not to have to watch out for the cars. There were some paths to follow. They could tell the news of what mom and dad were doing.

One day the little farm girl's Grandma had a little pig in a box in the kitchen. The mama pig didn't have room for it. Grandma gave it to her granddaughter. The lid kept coming off the shoe box and the little pig could run real fast before it was caught and put back in the box. Her dad said grandma should have put it in a gunny sack and would have been easier to bring home. The granddaughter had to feed it a bottle until it could eat from a trough. Dad built a little pen for it until it could go in with the big pigs. When this little pig became a mama and her pigs big enough for market, the little farm girl was given one to sell. Her dad couldn't have afforded for her to have sold her pig until it had pigs. She remembers the $13 she finally could have for all her work and remembers going to Schultz's Dept Store in Terre Haute to buy her first coat. It was a princess style wool with many little knobs of color with lots of blue and purple. Wow! A coat that she didn't have to stand still for fittings when her mom would poke her shoulders and make her stand up straight to measure the hem! Wearing that coat made her know that waiting for the first little pig to be a mama pig was worth it. The coat was not thrown away when she outgrew it.

Years later when she had a little girl of her own, her mother decided to cut the coat down and made a coat for her granddaughter. It was to be just a play coat and it was made long to keep her warm while she played outside or went with granddad to the barn. It was heavy and made good padding when granddad let her ride the cow. One day granddad put her in the car and went to the store. He was so proud of that homemade hand me down coat that he told the storekeeper lady, "Don't tell my wife I brought this little girl over here in this old long coat!" This granddad was always sneaking around with things he didn't want his wife to know.

This little granddaughter learned a lot from her grandfather. In only a few years, not quite five, he had taught her and did things she would never forget. He was the first to teach her to sing. A big song for such a little girl. And how surprised the family was when he proudly announced that Linda had a song to sing. Her little voice was sweet to his ears as she sang, "At the Cross At the Cross Where I First saw the Light and the Burdens of my Soul Rolled Away. It was There by Faith I received my Sight, and now I am Happy all the Day." He taught her what he believed, with a prayer that she would always remember.

Often the farm girl would remember how the pond at her grandma and grandpa Cox's looked big when she was a little girl. One evening, many years ago, she went over the hills and through the pasture to find her dad at the pond fishing. Her dad made a pole out of a strong stick and some cord with a safety pin for a hook. She was scared and surprised when her pole was almost pulled from her and dad had to help her. A turtle had taken the safety pin and she had to have help to pull it out of the water. It was big and ugly and a fighter but it was subdued and her dad carried it home like a hobo dangling from a big stick over his shoulder. It was getting dark but his wife hadn't lit the coal oil lamps yet. The little girl giggled as they went into the house and said, "Surprise!" Lighting the lamp the mother nearly dropped it when she saw the turtle. The giggling stopped when no one else was laughing. The dad was real proud of the catch and proceeded to dress it out for meat. The wife cooked the thing but no one thought she really put her heart into it and it didn't taste as gourmet as they had always heard turtle meat would be. It was a fun time for the little girl to spend with her dad and he was proud to provide a meal from the land.

Living on a farm was perfect for food on the table but there wasn't much cash. The livestock ate a lot of the hay and corn that was raised and the prices were low for what was available to be sold. A great shock in the cash flow occurred when there was an accident at the deep mine one winter when there was a cave-in of the roof of one of the coal veins. Slate fell and this enterprising young side-line farmer's ankle was broken, nearly broken off and almost hanging only by flesh and a couple bones. His family still remembers the Model A that pulled up and two men got out and made a criss cross hand sling and the dad sat with his arms around their necks as he was carried into the house. The men went on to Fontanet to get the doctor to come to the house to take care of the ankle. A bed was set up in the living room to make it close to the heating stove and this is where the ankle was examined. It would take a miracle to set this bone and for this man to walk again. Dr. Newlin performed that miracle and with tender loving care, the bone healed after many months on crutches. There was no income that winter after the accident but the mining company helped a little and maybe did pay for the doctor, which was probably twenty dollars.

Money problems became worse until there wasn't enough for the mortgage payment nor to pay the property taxes. Doom and gloom had set in and this couple realized they would lose their place. They began looking for cheaper places and were quite discouraged at the conditions of what they would be forced to get. One cheap place was a weathered little house back off the road on a rutty lane. The mother wasn't much to show emotion, but she went back to her nice new house on the mortgaged 40 acres and slumped in a rocking chair and cried. In the meantime, a neighbor friend had 20 acres across the road he wanted to sell for a very reasonable price. There was a financing plan that was new, called the School Fund. Payments were low on loans and interest was low. Knowing they would lose their farm fields and house, they took what money they had and made down payment on the 20 acres and planned to move in a box car or caboose which they could buy for not much. They would live in that. When his ankle healed enough that he could be on crutches, he got a job on the WPA that was a government-funded project that hired men to build roads and bridges. Until he could walk, he was the timekeeper that paid some cash for being on the job an hour of morning and an hour at night, and he also received some money for the use of a horse he had. The horse pulled a slip scraper which was a big iron scoop that scraped the roads to make the hills less steep. There were lots of jokes about those who worked on the road and people frowned when they saw a worker leaning on his shovel. When in fact, the worker often didn't take time to set down, but he sometimes did take a break and leaned on his shovel for support. And some people were too proud to work on the WPA, thinking it was a government handout. Better to work on WPA than starve with nothing to do. As the ankle improved to about normal, which was still a miracle that such an injury could improve so much, he worked all day using his horse and the slip scraper. The job ended when the road was finished. The WPA was what he needed to get some money to buy the twenty acres across the road from the forty acres and the house he built and loved so much. And his healed ankle put him back on his feet.

The same realtor who handled the twenty acres sale also knew about the school fund. When he learned of the plight that this young farmer and wife were about to lose their new house he devised a way for them to keep it. He called the banker who was foreclosing the 40 acres. He asked some casual questions about price, etc. and found the new asking price was far less than what the foreclosed couple owed. Money was scarce and there weren't any buyers. The realtor called the banker a few days later saying he might have a buyer and asked what the lowest price he would accept. The new figure was much lower and it was evident that the banker was anxious to sell to recoup some cash. He called the banker and told him he had a buyer. The realtor also said he had been to the courthouse and found that there were back taxes and his buyer didn't want to pay them. The banker was not happy and said, "Well didn't they even pay the taxes." The realtor said, he guessed not. The banker agreed to pay the taxes and told the realtor to proceed with the deal.

Much secrecy had taken place since the first day of the realtor saying he would like to help get the property back for the ones who deserved it with the house they had built, etc. No one was ever told of the possible negotiation, not even close relatives or the kids. A neighbor friend who recommended the realtor who knew about the School Fund financing, was a true friend and emphasized that no one must know for fear the banker would find out. These two neighbors had talked on many issues and subjects while they sat on a back porch many nights listening to their fox hounds. For several months there was complete secrecy even to the day of the signing of the deed in the office of the realtor. The banker sent his attorney which made it a little safer, however the "new-buying" couple was well hidden in another office until it would be time for them to sign their papers. The Doty's had already signed their Forfeit Papers to the bank. The banker's attorney and the realtor went over all the papers thoroughly and the attorney signed the deed for the banker that made binding the transfer to the new owners.

The couple was then asked to come in the office to sign as the new owners. When the banker's attorney saw his signed copy, he looked again at the papers and saw where Doty's had signed the foreclosure papers and also signed as the new owners. He actually was very pleased and shook their hands and congratulated them. He realized it was right for them because the ground was too high priced in the first place and the banker had already made enough profit from the payments that were made for many years. And the banker was being obstinate not to lower their payments and then showed he was willing to sell it to someone else for what it was worth. And he also would have gotten the house along with his overpriced ground. So guess what went around, comes around.

When it was known that the Doty's were keeping their farm and house and also had the 20 acres across the road, everyone was really glad for them. People in the country were like that. Their home never looked so good to this farmer and his wife and they were thankful they would remain in the neighborhood in the house that no one had lived in except them.

The one neighbor who had kept the secret, suggested a chicken roast as a way to celebrate. They chose a grassy area out by the orchard. They scooped a spot for a fire to be built of hickory limbs, put some metal posts in the ground and about four feet of clothesline wire across the poles. On the evening of the event, the fire was built and smelled so good. Neighbors were invited which made a crowd of about twenty five or so. The men dressed chickens and they were hung whole from the wire high enough over the embers to roast. Potatoes were laid along the edge of the fire to cook. Two long tables were made with boards laid over saw horses and the women brought bright printed table cloths. One table was for the carry-in dishes of macaroni and cheese, pickled beets, scalloped corn, green beans seasoned with jowl bacon, and about anything else these good country cooks could think of. The other table had benches alongside for people to sit to enjoy the food. These neighbors didn't live sixty years in this world for nuthin.

The farm girl parents realized that leaving town for the farm was a good move and meant to be. A Happy 25th Wedding Anniversary was celebrated with family and close friends. That morning of April 14, 1939 the "groom" was very proud of the bouquet of little purple violets he had picked while sitting in a snow bank. It was a very good day and their love was as new as it was on their wedding day in 1914.

He repeated his request that if possible he wanted a bouquet of wild woods flowers by his casket. His favorite were the Sweet Williams that bloom very early in the spring and have a heavenly fragrance His family thought about his request but it was a January many years later with cold and snow and no wildflowers.

AFTER PEARL HARBOR, THINGS WERE DIFFERENT

Everything started going better with money more plentiful and people busy and happy. December 7, 1941 changed lives forever. The United States was attacked at Pearl Harbor. The farm girl's cousin, Raymond Hollingsworth as soon as he graduated from Fontanet High School, enlisted and was there with the Marines during the attack. Immediately there was a mass registration of young men. Some waited to be drafted and some enlisted but nearly all young men and some women too, went to the service of their country. Seeing sons and brothers, daughters and sisters leave home to go to training camps was not a good experience. It was something everyone just had to get used to. It was the way of life at that time. The end of basic trainings were sombre times to see these young people in crisp uniforms coming home on furlough. Reunions with parents, aunts and uncles, grandmas and grandpas brought families together. When the precious days at home ended, everyone knew they would be shipped overseas. All tried to be brave when bidding farewell to those in uniform who had grown up in a hurry to be in the military service.

The farm girl's father put on the most pleasant face to bid his son goodbye. He just wouldn't let anyone look sad and everyone had to be cheerful. Later he could be seen going out behind the barn, no doubt to use his bandana to wipe a tear. While his son went overseas, first to North Africa, to Sicily, Italy and France, he had a positive attitude and made letters sound cheery. He wrote about things when his son would be back home again.

His son sent money home regularly and it was saved for him to use when he got home. It would have been a surprise when he was coming home, except there was a list of men printed as they landed in New York and someone saw his son's name on the list in a New York Times. Four days later the son, Howard, walked in grinning from ear to ear and everyone acted surprised. No words can say how this family felt that the war was ending and the country would be at peace again. People were reunited, ties renewed and love bonded with roots deep in hearts and souls of everyone. The farm girl's brother was surprised to know there was money in the bank for him. He used this $3800 money to start the Black and white Cab Company in Mattoon.

One neighbor mother couldn't be consoled from sadness that her son was fighting overseas. She was a good Christian woman. She often said that she knew her son wouldn't come home. He didn't and it surely wasn't her lack of faith, but maybe a premonition. It was sad for neighbors to see their young men's pictures in the paper as announcements of killed in action were made, including Lawrence Stewart and James Wells. Several of the area young men didn't make it home but most of them did.

CHURCH AND WORSHIP

Church stuff was the thing the farm family just did. It didn't have to be a cathedral or building with a steeple to be a church. There were two churches in Fontanet, the Church of God and the Catholic Church, both well attended. Harvey and Laura Cox thought a long time and felt the need to establish a third church. They read books of doctrines of various denominations and chose to be founders of the Fontanet United Brethren. The doctrine had qualities and beliefs they felt suited them and the community. The main one being that no United Brethren would coax or try to influence any other church member to leave a church and join the United Brethren. The basics also included United Brethrens could never tell any other church person that their faith was wrong. Being respectful and tolerant of all faiths appealed to the basis of the third church. There was no building but a group who wanted another church. Several charter members joined the founders to establish the church. The Knight of Pithians Lodge leased the first floor of their building for a minimal charge. The United Brethren Conference issued a charter and supplied a minister. Services were held there for many years, maybe 20. The desire for a church building was met with diligent prayer and hard work. There was a bachelor, Ralph Hollingsworth, whose folks had operated a grocery and feed store and he took it over after they died until he wanted to retire. He donated the building and 3 acres for a new church. The members dismantled the old building and saved the bricks for the church. Members put money in the building fund and agreed to a small mortgage loan to buy the hardwood for the floor and the stained glass windows. On the dedication day the church was filled and a day-long service with carry-in dinner was a day to remember. During the afternoon singing service, a financial report was read. Times were hard and cash was scarce. Hands went up for pledges of $10, $25 and $50 to be paid in six months to pay off the mortgage. The farm girl's father pledged $100 and his family wondered where in the world it would come from. Somehow the money came and the pledge was honored.

The Church of God had many members who were friends of the United Brethrens. When the United Brethren founder became too ill to attend church, it was his old friends from the Church of God who came to his house and had prayer meetings on summer Thursday evenings and sang songs to make his last days on earth as close to Heaven as they could be until his death in 1936.

The founders of the Fontanet United Brethren church lived down a long lane off the Rio Grande pavement in rural Brazil Indiana with six daughters until two sons came along. The house is remembered as being a living room and a parlor across the front and step down into a long kitchen with a bedroom off to the left. There was a roofed concrete walkway from the kitchen to a summer kitchen. With that large family there were beds in all rooms except the kitchen. There was a wood/coal cooking range in the kitchen used in cold weather and another stove in the summer kitchen. There was a fireplace in the living room and a small potbelly stove that used the same flue. In summer the stove was pushed back even with the fireplace. There was a big bed in the living room, a serpentine dresser, a library table with a coal oil lamp and two rocking chairs. When company came, chairs were brought in from the kitchen.

It was the custom that whichever child caught the chicken got the gizzard. One Sunday the preacher was asked home for dinner. As soon as the preacher said the blessing Amen, he also looked at the plate of chicken and said in his robust manner, "And look at that – my favorite piece of chicken," and he forked the gizzard to his plate. The mother could see the disappointment in her little girl's face and probably a secret pact that she would get the gizzard the next time for sure somehow. The six sisters and two brothers were shown love and respect and they returned love and respect to their parents. The children were just like kids though and they had their disagreements and spats and did some arguing. They also looked out for one another. If one did something to another that wasn't right or was hurtful, another sister or brother would interfere or plan a suitable revenge. They didn't tattle but had their own system of solving disagreements. They respected parents and would quit the argument as soon as a parent appeared. The farm girl remembers her mother telling about the fun playing baseball. She said they used a board to bat the ball that was made out of rags. It took awhile to cut the rags in strips and wind them round and round tight in a ball. She could never figure out how her grandchildren could hit a ball with such a little "stick" bat.

The Fontanet United Brethren church founders had a big orchard of apple trees, pear trees, peach trees, and grapes. In 1928 the agriculture class at the Fontanet high school was studying orchard tree pruning and needed an orchard to give some practical experience. Orville Redenbacher was the teacher and he took his class several times until the orchard was pruned to perfection. His whole class probably got an A and they didn't know until many years later that Orville Redenbacher would become a giant in the popcorn industry. One of these students didn't know until many years later that his son would marry the orchard owner's great granddaughter

TO JOHNNIE AND LINDA,
April 15. 1977, by Mom Taylor

A tribute to the Anniversary (April 15, 1972)
Of twenty five years, since the couple said I Do.
Linda Jean Taylor and Johnnie Harold Devereaux
Solemnly declared their intent to establish a home.

At the Fontanet Bean Dinner, about August 1968,
At ages 18 and 14, they had their first "date."
Around the grounds they walked hand in hand;
Four years later to be wearing wedding bands.

Johnnie left the rural area for Indy the next day;
He'd drive to the big city to be a barber some day.
Then he'd sail around the world with the US Navy:
Linda back to Illinois to cheer on the Mattoon Wave.

January 1972, beloved Grandma Taylor passed away
And Johnnie was there for Linda, words of comfort to say.
At that time, Aunts and Uncles noticed and said,
"He's so kind, some day those two will wed."

Lara's Theme played as the mothers were seated,
Eileen by Deb, and Norma by Granny Doty, so sweet.
Brothers Tracy and Steve, ages 10 and 12, candles lit,
As the Terre Haute Locust Street Church was made all fit.

The organ played as Linda, with dad to be given away,
Smiled at Papa John and Bessie on a perfect day.
Reverend Loveall heard their vows of love;
Prayed their home be blessed from Heaven above.

And their home was blessed and made sublime,
A son, Dane Matthew, born November 24, 1979.
Now a family entrusted to His watchful care,
As promising as Over the Rainbow Somewhere!

A FAMILY IN THE LATE 1890'S AND HOW THEY GREW

A family with eight children on a farm learned to be frugal and almost self-sustaining. Mothers would buy a bolt of material to make dresses. Common was outing flannel for winter. Children wore those dresses to school and took them off as soon as they came home to put older ones on to do their chores or to even just eat and be around the house. Buying by the bolt was cheaper than having it pieced out. Wall paper almost always had shades of red and pink and girls sneaked behind a door and would wet their fingers and rub against their favorite shade of pink or red and then rub on their cheeks to liven the color of their skin. They learned how to blend it at the edges so as not to make them gaudy or cheap looking. Six girls probably made lots of rubbed spots and that is another reason they used the wall paper behind the door that wouldn't show.

One time the two youngest girls were about to be misbehaving and the mother told a story about wet hair couldn't be cut. That same afternoon the little girls were just as mischievous as they could be and their mother told them, "You have not been doing as you were told and have not been listening when I've said no. Go get the scissors and I am going to cut your hair." Well even the youngest girls loved their long hair and had been taught that girls with short hair might be looked down upon. It was just the beginning of the flappers and they had heard enough that they didn't think they wanted to be one. The older sisters remembered hearing that wet hair was hard to cut so they told the misbehavers to hurry and put their heads in the rain barrel. Of course the bigger sisters had to help hold the little sisters who used a dipper to reach down in the barrel. This was sisterhood in the utmost and showed they looked out for one another. The farm girl's grandmother was like that. She used psychology for discipline and no one ever remembered any spankings. Wonder how many years for these kids to figure out that wet hair really could have been cut easily and wasn't it funny that their mother told the story in the midst of the misbehaving.

When the oldest sister, Flora, had been away, probably when she was a student in Greencastle Indiana at DePauw College in the late 1890s, the little sisters were excited when they saw her coming up the lane to visit home. One ran to meet her and hugged her around the knees and then made playful circles all around her and was singing, "It's a secret that we are having fried chicken for supper. But we can't tell." Flora acted surprised and no one ever knew little sister Alice had sung her the secret.

One time a sister didn't agree with her mother and went to the barn to talk to her father about it. He patiently listened and then said, "Just do as your mother says." Probably just listening to herself and hearing it out loud made her know that her mother was wise and kind. Her father knew that and if he didn't agree it would be discussed without children hearing.

Coming home on cold afternoons the children would look forward to the black iron pot on the wood stove steaming with hot mush. Eating it with cream must have been delicious. The mush left over was cooled and sliced for breakfast to be fried in the iron skillet with bacon grease for flavor. How wonderful with syrup made from the sap of the maple trees. Wood hollow spigots were drilled into the trees. When the winter thaws started, so did the sap in the maple trees. Buckets were put under the spigots to catch the sap. The sap was put in a kettle and put on the back of the stove to evaporate the water to the consistency of syrup. Took a lot of sap to make a gallon of syrup but it was worth the effort and made the house smell yummy through the month of February.

It was a family affair when the wagon was hitched up to a team of horses. In winter, straw was placed in the wagon and the kids would dig themselves a cave in the straw and cover up with homemade comforts to keep the straw from blowing out. They went to church often this way in winter and sometimes even to Fontanet or to Terre Haute, which was an all day roundtrip. There might have been a buggy the family could have rode by sitting on laps or hanging on. In winter the wagon was much warmer and two horses could pull more. Kids liked to go to the mill with sacks of wheat and corn to be ground for flour or meal. It was in North Terre Haute called Markle's Mill. It was on a creek that was dammed with a concrete spillway. Kids used to think it was like pictures of Niagara Falls. School was on the Rio Grande pavement not far from the farmhouse that set off the road about half a mile. It was called the Hoffman School probably because the ground was provided by the farmer who owned the land.

About a month before one Christmas, the two little boys strayed from their usual good behavior. They were almost impish and were warned that if they didn't improve, that Santa Claus would not come. They ignored the warnings and kept on being bad as they could be. An older sister had gone to a church program and a bag with oranges, peanuts and candy was handed out as the usual church Christmas treat. When she got home she saw two plates setting out on the table next to the fireplace in the room where she was to sleep. Everyone was in bed. Nothing was in the plates that were left for Santa Claus to leave something. She felt so bad that she put an orange in each plate and some peanuts. The next morning she was awake when she heard the little boys tip toe and saw them sneaking a look at their plates. Her heart was warmed as she saw them clap their hands and whisper, "He did come. He did come. Santa Claus did come!" They didn't know their big sister had done this for them. This sister was a petite 5 ft 1 inch and weighed 90 pounds.. She was at the age she could be courting. She delighted having her dashing beau carry her across the branch after a hard rain and water covered the hardpan dirt lane. When beaus came the couple could sit in the parlor. The farm girl's mother told her they called it sparking. The coal oil lamp chimney would be washed bright and clean so the room would look the best possible. She chose the special one and they courted four years. Sometimes he borrowed a car from someone wealthy in Burnett to come to rural Brazil when he didn't rent a horse and buggy from the livery stable.

The two young brothers turned from their impish ways and grew to be fine young men. The little brothers liked to hunt and fish with their sister's new husband. The youngest boy became ill with sugar diabetes. He was sick about two years and was seventeen when he grew weaker. He read a lot, including the Bible. His Christian parents had instilled traits in him of which they were very proud. One day as his mother was tenderly caring for him, Herbert looked at her and said, "Mom, I have learned about Heaven and I know it will be beautiful and wonderful. There will be only one thing wrong, that you won't be there with me." Hiding a tear she said, "Son, just not for awhile." He died in 1922 which was about a year before insulin was available.

The big yard was fenced and as new trees were planted along the edge, they were named for each of the eight children. When these children left home to be married and came back with their kids, they were proud to see how their tree was doing. It was sweet that the tree named for Herbert was Tree of Heaven. It was a comfort to see that tree as it grew and lived to an old age. The yard had corners of hollyhock flowers, gooseberry bushes, dewberry plants, snowball bushes, lilacs and honeysuckle. There was an open front porch with tubs of huge hydrangea that were carried to the cellar in cold weather and brought out again in the spring.

The other son told about being in Terre Haute when two women approached him outside the Woolworth Dime Store. They started a conversation with him when he was about twelve years old and gave him a pamphlet to read. They were representing the Women's Christian Temperance Union and were telling people about the dangers of drinking alcohol. He listened and when asked to sign a pledge card that he would never drink any alcoholic drinks, he signed the card. He said he never forgot that he had signed the card. Although he was raised by parents who founded a church and he went to church when living at home, later somehow found himself too busy or too indifferent to attend church when he had a family.

He had good children that went to church. When it was just he and his wife at home, he started occasionally attending various services and at the close of a service during an invitation song, "Just as I am I Come," he was filled with the desire to become what God wanted him to be. He went to the altar with deep remorse that he had not been as close to God as he should have been. He also knew he needed forgiveness and a new direction for his life. He was saved. He also realized that if he had not signed that WCTU pledge card, that he probably could have been a real scoundrel. He soon felt a calling to be a lay minister and he made his mark of Christian endeavor for several years in churches that he worked with. He worked with youth groups and his skillful ability to roller skate kept him active until he was about 80. He planned skating parties for church young people. On the rink you couldn't tell him from one of the kids. There wasn't much he couldn't do and he thought it stemmed from hearing his father say over and over, "Can't never did anything."

Grandkids remember going to grandpa and grandma's. They remember hearing their mothers telling of one April Fool's Day they pretended that someone had called on the crank telephone and wanted grandpa. They went out to the barn and told him to come to the house to talk on the phone. He was a big man, and probably starting to get old, and he had to quit what he was doing and walk all the way to the house. When he got there his kids hollered that it was an April Fool Joke. He didn't laugh and no one ever did that again. He was a kindly, gentle man who was pretty serious. Grandma was the jolly one and mixed fun with being serious. She was smart too and could work the crossword puzzles. She could always tell the kids how to spell and help with arithmetic. She had more schooling than grandpa, perhaps a year of college at the University of Illinois. She is remembered for her way of disciplining. A granddaughter remembers her mother, Eva, telling a story about David, who was the first boy of seven children. When he was close to three years old, he had developed the habit of throwing "fits" or in a modern day would be called tantrums. David was on the floor kicking and screaming. His mother leaned over and very softly, so low that he had to quit screaming to hear, said to him, "Honey, will you just scoot over under the table so someone won't step on you." The little boy didn't know what else to do, so he just got up and scampered away, probably deciding that his fit got him nowhere and no extra attention for sure.

Story was told that the farm girl's Grandpa Cox ventured to Illinois in a horse and buggy. That was a long drive so it would be an overnight trip to visit a friend. Coming back it was beginning to get dark and he somehow took a wrong road and was lost. He was worried that he wasn't going to make it back to rural Brazil Indiana as he would be expected. There were no places to inquire directions. It was very dark when he came to a little town and saw dim lights in a building. It was a jail. He went in and the sheriff realized his plight and invited him to spend the night with a warm meal and a cell. Leaving as early as he could the next morning, he found the right road and when he got home their grandma was so delighted. Grandpa wasn't away from home much, if ever. She grabbed him and hugged him and they went around laughing in a circle. Grandpa knew he needed an explanation for being a day late. He told her he had gotten lost and spent the night in a jail BUT she was warned not to tell anybody. Grandpa didn't want anyone to know. Grandma thought it was funny and she did tell.

Another story remembered by the farm girl's cousin, Sarah, when grandpa wanted to venture out west to seek his fortune. He had heard there was wealth there to be had. He started making plans to go when grandma very explicitly informed him, "No you are not going and leave me here with all these yungins!" He didn't go.

All of the grandchildren loved to spend time on the farm at their grandparents. Some would spend weeks at a time before they had to go to school and the house was always full in summers. One time three or four of them were playing and were ages four to seven. An older boy, one of the Green neighbors, was visiting and he threw Raymond's slingshot high in the air and it landed near to the top of the silo. He started crying and his little sister, Hazel, wanted to comfort him. She said, "Don't cry. I will go up and get it." Her little legs just barely reached from rung to rung up the ladder on the side of the big silo. She was about half way down when her mother and grandma came flying out of the house. They wrung their hands until she was safely down, then scolded her for climbing that dangerous big silo. No one that young had ever climbed it before so that made Hazel proud!

One time just after dark the dogs were barking up a storm, like Grandpa Cox had ever heard before. He tried to see what they were barking at but It was so dark he couldn't see. He decided the dogs were just barking at a possum or raccoon. The next morning early grandma had breakfast on the table and they had just said the "Amen" after grace when they heard the front screen door open. Someone walked through the front room and stepped down into the kitchen. Grandma saw him first and she said, "Well, it's Lewis." And grandpa said, "Where did you come from?" Lewis was a grandchild, one of the older ones. Lewis said he got there last night but it was dark and the dogs were barking. He was close to a tree so he climbed the tree and the dogs seemed not friendly as they barked and barked. He decided it safer to stay in the tree. By the time the dogs went away he was asleep. He soon found a spot at the table and ate the sausage and gravy and buttermilk biscuits.

The 1945 junior girl at Fontanet High School, has had a wealth of memorable stories shared. Lewis's sister, Sarah wrote a letter dated December 20, 2003. "Dear Norma Mae, It is a beautiful sunny day and I am so glad to see road ice is melting. I've enjoyed your phone calls so much and am enclosing something that I will be watching to see that it is cashed. Part of it is for being included in the floral sympathy for our dear cousin Rose

Mary and it has taken me a year to send. Some is to be used for your time spent to do your book, your first book.

Today is the first official day of winter and I already have had enough. But Grandpa Cox knew snow is the poor man's fertilizer. So he could have prayed: Lord, give us snow just as you know is best for us. Give courage and strength and wisdom to cope with our inconveniences, knowing as you do, that our beans will be greener, wheat more golden, apples rosier, and corn kernels fatter, if these flora are well-nourished. His beautiful little girls, on hot days, brought him cold water in the special battered covered pail. They waited at the edge of the plowing or discing field, under a tree or bushes until he would come for a turn around. His heart was filled with deep love as he took off each bonnet and brushed back the sweaty wisps of thin or uneven brown hair. His fingers were strong and rough – but oh! They caressed as truly lovingly. Their names were like bright gemstones in his large heart. The children held him in honor and they knew he loved their mother, a great legacy! God's plan for family cohesion!" Norma Mae deposited the check and it will have paid for a copy of any first book.

GROWING IN FAITH

The churches in Fontanet touched the lives of many folks. At the United Brethren church during a revival of weeklong services, many people made decisions to join the church or dedicate themselves to the work of the church for the Lord.

The little farm girl was six years old and during the invitation song, "Softly and Tenderly I Come," she went to the altar and said she wanted to be a member. She was welcomed and the congregation pledged to support this little one. When she was twelve she had a little Sunday school class of four and five year olds. In the far left corner of the first floor of the KP building that was used as the church, there was a table with little chairs. These children listened as she read to them and she helped them learn their recitations for the Easter and Christmas programs. She had been trained by her mother how to say a piece or recitation. She wasn't allowed to sound sing-songy. She had to put her hands behind her so she wouldn't fiddle with her dress hem, raise her head high, open her mouth wide and pronounce each word loud enough to be heard in the far corner of the church. She could have written a chapter in a book for public speaking. The mother taught her to sing in much the same manner. There was a revival at the church when she was about seven years old and the evangelist had a choir of eight or nine children. They had memorized the words because some were too young to read so none had a song book. Whether it was a recitation or a song, the little farm girl had been taught not to mumble and to look out over the audience so they could hear. The evangelist tried hard not to laugh during the first verse and he did motion with his finger to his lips but she just kept singing the words, "Sowing in the morning, sowing seeds of kindness, Sowing in the noontide and the dewy eve; Waiting for the harvest, and the time of reaping, We shall come rejoicing bringing in the cheese." And the chorus, "Bringing in the cheese, bringing in the cheese, We shall come rejoicing, bringing in the cheese". And this being a farm community everybody knew it should be Bringing in the Sheaves. Like wheat or shocks of corn at harvest. She either was looking out at the audience and not at the evangelist, or she didn't understand the finger to his lips because she sang the three verses and the chorus three times. Singing loud and enunciating each word plainly, including "Bringing in the Cheese."

When she was fourteen there was a United Brethren camp conference for teens at Indianapolis on a small college campus. The church congregation agreed to sponsor two teens to this camp. One at the last minute backed out, but the other agreed to go. The minister and his wife drove the 60 miles to take her. A feeling of apprehension to be up there "alone" was almost overwhelming but soon subsided as she was shown her dorm room and met three roommates who were in their mid teens also. They happened to be from a church in Terre Haute, about fourteen miles from Fontanet.

Unpacking was fun as they showed their new outfits and told about what was fun at home to do. There was some serious talk too. These Terre Haute girls talked about they had just been saved, had been to the altar to ask for forgiveness and were saved! This Fontanet girl was a little disappointed in these three city girls and wondered what they had done to have to be forgiven. She thought maybe they had smoked cigarettes.

There were classes and Bible study, meals in the cafeteria and evening vespers. The church chapel on campus was huge with a big balcony. There was a young man about 16 that the Fontanet girl had met and he talked about how he, too, had been saved... He and the Fontanet girl made plans to sit together one night at vespers. The two of them went to the farthest top corner of the balcony. The pulpit looked very small from up there. The writer is sure they went up there to giggle. There were lively hymns and some familiar choruses sung that church kids all knew. The minister started his sermon and in just a few minutes he had a captive audience, everyone was quiet including the two in the farthest top corner. Each word seemed to outline events in their lives. Told the story of how God so loved the world that he gave his only begotten Son that whosoever believeth in Him should not perish but have everlasting life. The minister explained there were two choices, to perish or be saved. There was that word again, "saved!" The minister invited those who had not been saved or who wanted to rededicate themselves to come forward as the song "Just As I Am" was sung. Several rose from their seats and the Fontanet girl was among the first. She felt as if she was sublimely alone and her inner feelings were turned to silver like a soft cloud. She knew she was being talked to by Jesus and happiness flooded her so deeply that she felt it in her chest. So happy she had tears and then she found herself at the altar in the very front of the church. She noticed the young man accompanied her and the three roommates met her at the altar, all happy to embrace her and kneel to pray with her. She was converted or turned around in her ways of thinking and truly knew she had accepted Jesus as her personal Savior This teen had been a member of the church since she was six and now she was saved, another plateau reached in her Christian growth.

The farm girl knew being saved didn't make her perfect but it made her mistakes easier. When taught by caring parents and Sunday school teachers, right from wrong is known. These teachings are a yardstick to measure as the standard so one can tell how far to the right or left a situation can be. Knowing she could pray to ask what she should do and pray to say she made a mistake and was sorry, made life a lot happier.

Grover and Alice Doty were proud of their daughter who had been to the camp conference and learned so much, made new friends and made her decision to have Jesus as her Savior. They were charter members of the Fontanet United Brethren church. He had a Sunday school class of about a dozen boys. He was a tall thin man with a waist size of 28 all his years and had been a telegraph operator on the railroad, worked in coal mines and was a member of the United Mine Workers, had a small farm, was a carpenter during the war to construct War Aid Depot, and worked on the Pennsylvania Railroad in the roundhouse because of labor shortage during the war. What he did, he did good. He was proud of his first social security check when he was sixty five in September of 1955.

The farm girl's daughter, Linda, when she was 4 years old, was taken by her grandmother to visit her great aunt. Next door was a barn and the farmer was shearing his sheep. The little girl was fascinated to watch for more than an hour. A couple days later the grandmother answered the phone to hear, "Do you know what happened? Well, let me tell you. My cat has been gone for two days. I called it and it didn't come. This morning it was at the back door and I wondered where it had been. It was probably too scared and embarrassed and stayed away until it was really hungry this morning. It looks terrible. Poor thing! It's fur has been cut on one side plumb down to its skin." She had a lot of agitation in her voice and seemed completely flustered. The grandmother was chuckling and asked, "Well, what do you think happened?" "Well don't you know what happened?" Your granddaughter did it!" crossly replying. "Well, you might be right as now I remember Linda did watch the sheep being sheared. But looks like we would have seen her come in the house to get the scissors." The grandmother laughed but soon stopped when she realized the phone call was not a social call. The poor cat's owner couldn't see any humor and certainly didn't think it was a laughing matter! Aunt Eva didn't stay mad too long at her little great niece

Springtime on the farm was highlighted by mushroom hunting. Certain spot's identity would be kept secret as long as possible. The big yellow morels were so delicious and quite a prize to find. One day the grown farm girl's father was repairing a fence. His little granddaughter was playing along the edge of the woods quite a distance away. Suddenly the little girl yelled, "Granddad, Granddad, come here quick!" Dropping the fence stretchers he hurried to see what was the matter. "Look here, look here, what is that little thing?" How her eyes spotted that small thing, granddad didn't know. He told her it was a little mushroom just peeking through the leaves. They looked around and found several more and some were bigger. How good they would taste with some scrambled eggs, maybe even for dinner. These were the smaller black sponge ones and they would be followed a week later by the big really meaty yellow ones.

The farm girl's dad knew where he could always find the big ones. It was across the branch in the pasture and up a steep hill. He was not too happy one morning at the store, when the storekeeper grinned and said he had found a big hatful of morels. Questioned him where and by the look of guilt he knew why he himself had not found any in the prized spot. Didn't hesitate to ask if he could come in the store and take loaves of bread or cookies? Wide eyed the store keeper soon got the message! Mushrooms are the Cadillac's of delicacies

He was just a little mad about the mushrooms but didn't stay that way long. The Beshaw's had a good grocery store which was very convenient and only a half mile walk. When the farm girl's mother had extra ten cents she would buy minced ham for a sandwich which was a treat over the usual plain old country sausage. Or she would fry it in bacon grease and make gravy which had a different flavor than regular old sausage gravy, which was also very tasty. Store bought lunch meat was something to look forward. The mushroom patch owner was forgiving even though he was awhile forgetting, but a lasting friendship between a storekeeper and this customer was unwavering. Several years later the farm girl went into the store with her Norwegian friend She picked up a bag of Chesty Potato Chips and two bottles of Orange Whistle and waved to the storekeeper. He nodded and out she went. The Norwegian friend looked at her most perplexed. The girl said, "Oh, on Thursdays we don't have to pay"... and then she told him that the storekeeper would write it down on her dad's grocery bill. Most everyone ran a bill and paid it periodically on payday or when chickens were sold, or when a load of hogs were taken to market.

A FAMILY VACATION

In August of 1955 the farm family, Grover and wife, Alice and their daughter and granddaughter, Linda, and their son, Howard, took a trip. Howard was a professional truck driver and he drove the pretty blue 1953 Ford over mountains in Yellowstone Park like the pro he was. Such sights as never they had seen and so many pictures of the bears that came right up to the car and Old Faithful made this a vacation of a lifetime. An aunt and uncle lived in Billings and they knew all about Yellowstone. The aunt was going to go with them and they had reservations for two nights in a cabin by Fishing Bridge. The dad didn't know how much the cabins would cost but hid a fifty dollar bill in his billfold. He wanted to pay for the cabins but was told not to worry about it. Turned out the cost was two dollars a night. Aunt Edith insisted they take warm clothes to the park and was a little aggravated when some shorts and tee shirts were packed. The first night was a little chilly in the double cabin and the fire in the iron stove didn't take much hold. Throughout the next day they accumulated some bits of paper and some evergreen twigs. The truck driver prided himself in getting a fire started, boy did he ever! The cabin soon was hot, very hot and the only nightclothes were warm ones of flannel. The door had to be opened so they could even breathe. Bears were outside getting into scrap food that had been put in trash barrels. It was a choice of breathing or not.. so the door had to remain open and the fire builder who was on the floor in a sleeping bag, slept with one eye open to make sure bears didn't come in the cabin. Everyone got the giggles, including the aunt who was normally very serious. The more they tried to be quiet, the more someone would think of something to laugh about until the people in the second part of the double cabin had to repeatedly bang on the walls. The last day was hot and the pictures taken with the Kodak show people in shorts picking flowers by snow banks, show the family sitting on fir logs watching Old Faithful, show a bear with its nose 10 inches from the passenger side of the car, and some buffalo. This was the trip for this Hoosier family never to forget. It was just meant to be.

In September 1955 just before his 65th birthday, the farm girl's dad made a remark that he wished he had some money to go to Rockville to a sale and buy some feeder pigs. He had a field of corn picked and would only need to repair the fence. His daughter heard him and she asked how much he needed. She had a $100 bill stashed away with other money in the top door of the old pump organ. She said, "Here is what you need so it will just be a birthday present." He was so proud to turn those pigs lose in the cornfield. They run and rooted and feasted on the dropped ears or grains of corn. One morning before he went to Sunday School he looked out and said, "Oh just look out there at all the little cornpickers!"

Three days later in January this loving father had a heart attack. In the Brazil hospital his son kept hoping and saying as he referred to General Dwight D Eisenhower who had survived a heart attack, "Ike made it so maybe dad will." He didn't. He was handsome as he lay in his casket. His family had not realized he had such thick shiny silver hair. He had gotten older without anyone noticing.

Two nights of visitation and the Thomas funeral home was filled with friends and relatives. The list for the funeral procession was the immediate family behind the hearse followed by his brothers and sisters, his wife's brother and sisters, and 38 nieces and nephews from both sides of the family, cousins and friends. At the visitations hundreds of kin and friends and neighbors came to comfort the family. The brother introduced his sister to his truck-driver friends and proudly said, "This is my kid sister, she's 10 years younger than me." Didn't take her long to tell him he was writing 29 all over her! The brother and wife Ginny had a son, Jim, who was adored. Jimmy called him Pop Doty. His only granddaughter, who was almost five years old, had been to funerals and on the steps of the funeral home she said, "I can't wait to see Granddad in his pretty bed." It was good she knew what to expect. She had been taught to put her hands behind her at visitations and funerals when she looked at the flowers. This time her mother told her that the flowers were for Granddad and she could touch them and let them help her not to be sad. She was so sweet as she intently looked at the flowers and tenderly touched them and smiled as she smelled them. It helped her remember the good times and fun she had with granddad.

At the cemetery when the shiny black hearse stopped, there were about a dozen little boys ages eight to eleven that formed two lines making an aisle to the grave. The boys each were given a basket of flowers to hold while the casket was carried to the grave. No one knew this Sunday school class would be there. The young preacher, Max Powers, and the Sunday school superintendent had gone to school and asked permission to take them to the cemetery. What a tribute to their Sunday school teacher and how much the family appreciated it, never to be forgotten. Made this cold January day much warmer. The funeral was two days before his granddaughter's birthday. The family was still numb and sad and hadn't planned anything until she woke up and said, "Where's my birthday?" There was a phone call made to her granddad's brother, Clay Doty, and asked if they could come and bring some granddaughters. Didn't take long to get some cupcakes baked and some balloons blown up. They probably brought Jennifer and Peggy Fulmer. It is not remembered if their sisters, Barbara and Margaret came. This fifth year birthday party was a celebration that gladdened the hearts of those who mourned.

CITY FRIENDS AND DOCTORS

The three girls and their families from Terre Haute that were at the church camp in Indianapolis became friends with the Fontanet girl. They enjoyed visiting and doing things country kids did. They were good singers and often sang special songs for the Fontanet church services and also the church in Terre Haute. One time the country girl took the three city girls back thru the woods, over the crick and up the hills to see where her grandparents had lived. They thought it was just wonderful to wade in the water and to pick a big bouquet of snowballs. They had a Kodak and took pictures that kept the memories of that day.

When the Fontanet girl was a sophomore in high school, she had appendicitis and was in a hospital in Terre Haute. The hospital was short of beds because of an explosion that injured several sailors that were taking training at the college. No one in the family had ever been in a hospital either to be operated on or to visit anybody. Before and after visiting hours the mother took a bus to stay with one of these families. She mentioned how lonesome her daughter was in the hospital. She said she was in a room with a woman who had throat surgery and couldn't talk, another old woman who had long hair and sat in bed looking out the iron slatted high bed rail so she wouldn't wonder away. The city mother could not understand a country girl being lonesome that could enjoy hearing the cars down on the street and seeing the nurses. The country mother was quick to defend country life by reiterating a long list of activities country kids did. She told how busy her daughter was with school, coming to town on weekends to the show, busy playing in the band and going to ballgames, busy with 4H... mentioning every possible activity she could think of. The city mother said, "I would not have thought that." Eight days in the hospital was a long time for a busy teen. Cars were better after the appendicitis operation than they were when the farm girl had her tonsils out ten years before. Her dad took her home in his 1932 Chevy. Her recuperation was slow and she was still eating the broth diet when she got home until she went to the doctor to get her bandages off. Telling him how anxious she was to eat again, he asked why. He said she could have been on a regular solid diet the third day after the operation. Too bad nobody put it on her hospital chart the rest of the days she was there. She liked to eat and was tall and skinny already.

The girl with appendicitis remembered the new pink silk pajamas and how excited she was about having an operation to get her tonsils taken out. She wore the pajamas out in the yard and danced while she made up words to a song. That was before she got in the doctor's office and the nurse started to put the ether cup over her mouth and nose and told her it would smell and taste like orange juice. It didn't take a second for the little girl to figure out that was not true and she cried and squirmed causing ether to get in her eyes before it put her to sleep. The sore throat afterwards was pain she had never had before. She was taken from the doctor's office to her aunt Rosie's in Terre Haute just in case something didn't go right. The doctor thought she would be excited about eating ice cream. She wasn't. She never cared much for ice cream and always was disappointed at birthday parties with ice cream and cake. Her aunt Rosie fixed warm soft macaroni in a thin sauce which was wonderfully soothing, and slipped right down that sore throat. She could have gone home on Friday but her cousin, Raymond, wouldn't be there with his Model T (it was the best car in the family) and it had good tight side curtains so air wouldn't get to her to give her a cold.

Most of the time people didn't go to doctors with ordinary things like stepping on a nail, or with burnt feet if you stepped in hot ashes, or if you skinned your knees. There was baking soda you could use on about anything. Stinky brown Cox'es Barbed Wire Liniment was wonderful for puncture wounds like stepping on a nail. The hole healed from the bottom so there wouldn't be any infection or a scar. There was a smelly salve called Porter's that worked good on bruises. Everyone learned to take about any kind of three weeds and make a juice for a bee sting. Guess it was known not to use three-leafed weeds for fear it would be poison ivy. One day the paper boy was collecting at a sweet little neighbor lady's house and a honey bee stung his elbow. She cut an onion and told him to rub it on the elbow and the onion juice was like magic to make it quit hurting. Any help on a dreadful bee sting was good to know and remember.

Splinters were the worst and often dug out with big needles. Sometimes a piece of fat pork was wrapped around it hoping to draw the splinter out. Happy was the kid that saw the splinter in the pork and knew it didn't have to be tortured with the needle.

A few months after the stay in the hospital with appendicitis, the farm girl's mother needed an operation. By then the family was more acquainted with what being and visiting in a hospital was like. The hospital was not crowded and her care was excellent and her operation so painless that it was over before she knew it. In fact the next morning she couldn't understand why her family wasn't there. The nurse told her visiting hours wouldn't be until 2 p.m. She said, "Oh no, my operation is today and my family is supposed to be here." The nurse told her the whole family had been there during and long after the operation was over yesterday. She felt the bandages and was glad she wasn't in pain and realized her operation was over. Her son had just come home after four years in the army quartermaster division. He had sent generous portions of his pay home and he was grateful his money was in the bank for him. He was proud to pay the hospital bill for his mother which was around a hundred and fifty dollars.

WHY WE ARE WHAT WE ARE

The farm girl's dad was a member of the Knights of Pythian Lodge. It was fun to go to the suppers they had for the families and there was music, usually a piano player and a saxophone player. Her dad liked to dance and he bragged about when he was young and went to dances it was the custom to put chalk on everyone's heels. If you were a good dancer, you didn't leave chalk marks on the floor. The men must have been light-footed and skimmed the floor as did their lady partners. He taught his daughter to dance in much the same manner. His wife didn't much care for dancing especially when the partners held each other real close. When the jitterbug became popular she rather enjoyed that. She didn't seem to mind when the girls wore their crinoline underskirts and the best dancers were twirled and pitched and sometimes their skirts went over their heads. She didn't like the slow dancing when a straw couldn't be put between the tightly held partners. Dad and daughter were delightful dancers to watch and he taught her good.

It is true our loved ones never leave us but remain forever in our thoughts each time we remember something they said or something they taught. When issues are talked about often enough and explanations made to explain with logic, valuable traits are instilled in children. One such father had many friends of various religious and ethnic backgrounds. These were deep feelings and deep rooted friendships.

Often the farm girl's dad would tell about when he was growing up he lived in the little town of Burnett where there were black people, lovingly referred to as the cullered. He worked at one of the grocery stores and made deliveries in a wagon. Customers had the old party lines to call orders. Or sometimes when someone walked to the store he would load their groceries and take them home. He would use the wagon to go to fields to pick up watermelons to be sold. He loved all these customers and many were black. They always welcomed him and he enjoyed many offers of fresh-baked bread or a bowl of hot soup or an apple off the tree.

He was born in this area after his father had built several houses there. The first time the carpenter hauled lumber and nails to the building site, he was approached to be told that it was a mistake to leave these materials unattended. He was told that they would be stolen or vandalized as had been the case in instances before. The carpenter asked who was most likely to do it. Not being told for sure, he went to the main area of the town and saw who was hanging around. He noticed three young men possibly in their mid or late teens. One seemed to be dominating the conversation. The carpenter walked up to them and with a greeting, "Well how are you guys today?" They looked surprised that this stranger wanted to talk to them. The carpenter said he was going to be building a house down the road apiece and was needing someone to sorta watch over the site with the lumber there, etc. The two boys looked at the third. The carpenter then also looked at the third and said, "How would you like to work for me? I could use someone to keep an eye on the lumber and also help unload and I might need some other help later." The boy's expression changed from surly to smiley. Without hesitation he said, "Yes! I will help you." A young boy and two of his buddies might have been turned from a life of crime to a life of being apprentices to a carpenter. There were no problems on that job or any other job the contractor carpenter had in this community of Burnett Indiana.

Several years later the carpenter's son took his five year old son to the village grocery store where he had worked. This story is being told to emphasize how it was way back then and how people got along. There was a tall, lanky, gray bearded man that was greeted with a hearty handshake and grins from ear to ear. They knew one another from many years before when the dad had made deliveries from the store. The men were laughing and talking. The little boy tugged on his dad's pant leg to get his attention and asked, "Dad, is that a Nigga?" It is a fact of the times that black people were referred to with slang and is very delicate to explain. The word taken from context could be interpreted according to the intent as referring to anyone who was not like themselves. Slang words may have not been flattering and could be offensive but if these words were used for distinction, the interpretation could be to denote affection instead of hostility. No doubt this little boy had heard the word and did associate it with black people. His daddy used this question to define the word so that his son would not forget. The bearded man slapped his knee and laughed as the two men looked at each other when the little boy asked the question. The little boy's dad said, "Son, this is one of the best men daddy has ever known. He truly is my friend." The little boy got his first lesson and there was no prejudice or misunderstandings in that family and color was not seen, just good people and good friends. Having grown up with this ethnic culture was a privilege for this little boy's daddy.

His daughter respected her parents and found pleasure in pleasing them. She knew how they felt about most things. She was taught that it was better to marry close to one's bringing up to help eliminate any cause of disagreement between a couple. Her dad had many friends who were Catholic and he respected them and their belief. He did see differences in religion as an obstacle as to how children would be raised, etc. He thought it best that Catholic marry Catholic and Protestant marry Protestant. He encouraged friendship with all religions and ethnics, but discouraged intermarriages because of possible unresolvable disagreements. His philosophy, why borrow any unnecessary problems. He believed in happy marriages and families that worshiped in their own way together and each one should be proud within their own. He will be remembered by saying if you are dating and you see something you are uneasy with, magnify it ten times and see if it can be lived with. If not, quit dating that one. He meant that after marriage, that issue would be ten times worse. He would say, "Better to leave a situation than continue and be sorry or break someone's heart or be heartbroken." He meant let your head rule your heart where there might be conflicts but still remain friends with those of other religions and ethnic backgrounds.

The farm girl felt loved and protected by her parents and when she was faced with a situation, she used her upbringing to help make the right decision. If she had strayed beyond what she had been taught, she would not have expected them to have yielded to her. If she had blatantly crossed the lines, to have broken the hearts of her parents, the farm girl can't imagine what her life might have been. She often sees parents with broken hearts and the lack of respect is "not like it used to be." If parents don't yield and accept, they are issued ultimatums and often parents do yield and condone or accept in order to keep peace within the family. The farm girl worries that children are not following the Ten Commandment to honor thy father and mother. When one thinks of the valuable lessons learned and remembers the happy times, loved ones are always in the midst. The farm girl's parents taught their children well. They did not live in this world for nuthin and surely goodness and mercy followed them all the days of their lives and they shall dwell in the house of the Lord forever!

SUNDAY SCHOOL MOTHER TEACHER

Another Fontanet United Brethren Sunday school teacher to be remembered had a class of teenage boys and girls. One Sunday she made an announcement that she was looking for someone else to teach her class. Disappointment and surprise was evident on the faces of these young people. "Why?" they asked. With a little hesitation she revealed that she was in the family way and she would be caring for the baby. Didn't take long for someone to say, "Oh, we'll take care of the baby here while you teach." And when the time came, they did. They held the baby, rocked her back and forth. This little baby girl listened to her mother teach from the Bible while being held, loved and protected in the arms of many little mamas and papas every Sunday morning.

The new baby farm girl had a brother who was ten years old. When he was born he was 6 pounds with bald head with just a little light fuzz, a very pretty baby. The mother expected the new baby to be just the same and didn't know what to think when the baby girl was nearly 9 pounds with lots of very dark hair and not as pretty. The new baby was loved just the same. The 4th of July expected baby was a month old when she was born 2nd of August. The mother called her son to come look at the new baby. She told him that she and daddy would still rock him and read to him and he could be their baby boy. He held the little baby's hand and looked at his mother real good and then he left. About an hour later he came back and said, "I've been thinking and thinking and think we should just call her the baby." A baby girl could never have had a better brother.

Several years later this same teacher came home from church one Sunday and noticed that one of her stockings had come loose from its garter and slipped below the knee all crumpled down near her ankle. A cousin's daughter happened to be there to see the embarrassment of the teacher who wondered how long the stocking had been down and who would have seen it. And to think she had been teaching her class which was at the front of the church on the stage area next to the podium. She supposed everybody saw her with her stocking down. Not long after that was Valentine's Day. In the mail came an anonymous large envelope addressed to her. It was a professionally drawn sketch with some hearts and the back of a woman all dressed up with a fancy hat and dress with hem just below the knee. And there was a rumpled stocking that filled one leg from the knee to the ankle! The verse went something like this: "As you teach your Sunday school class, you are always so pious, prim and neat; but next time maybe you better look down at your feet." This cousin's daughter worked at a Graphic company and she had this Valentine specially designed! This was a personalized masterpiece valentine and took awhile to figure out that Gertrude Johnson had it made where she worked.

This Sunday school teacher had a wonderful sense of humor, was very devoted, could be quite serious, was fun-loving, was tender and caring, loved her Lord Jesus, was a wonderful hard working farm wife, and the best mother possible to the little girl who had joined the church when she was six and had been saved when she was fourteen.

In the Good Old Sunshine Way was a hymn that went something like this: "Oh my mother went to glory long ago, for she traveled in the good old sunshine way, she would often sing it as she testified about it. And my father went to glory long ago, for he traveled in the good old sunshine way, it was never hard to find him for the path he left behind him, Was always in the good old sunshine way."

And this was a legacy these parents left because they had parents with the same heritage many generations back. The Fontanet church planned a baptismal service for a Sunday afternoon at Raccoon Creek. A spot had been chosen not far off the road where the water was about waist deep and in a shaded area among the birch trees. The girl who joined the church at age six was now reading Bible stories and bedtime stories to her two-year old daughter. Realizing she hadn't been baptized, this would be the time. This young mother waded into the water to the minister whose name was Dale Cottom. With a prayer and saying, "Now I baptize you in the name of the Father, and of His Son, and of the Holy Spirit" she was completely immersed. It was just for a moment, but long enough to make her realize she was thankful her grandparents had founded the church, that her parents were charter members, and the congregation had sent her to church camp where she was saved. Her baptism attained another plateau of what was pleasing to God for her own soul's needs to walk in His way.

As years went by, the Fontanet farm girl was transplanted in the Mattoon Illinois area. Her coveted church membership was transferred to the Loxa Presbyterian Church. Loxa is a little village in rural Mattoon with a white church and stained glass windows. The hardwood floors are rich in beauty and the aisles are protected with lush green carpet. The people there are friendly, sincere and it was comfortable for her new church home. After several years she was nominated, elected and ordained as an elder. The honor was accepted as an unexpected gift. The humility she felt as she participated in the first communion service as an elder, was unexplainable. Being seated on the front pew and have the pastor bless the bread and the wine and then hand the trays to the elders to pass to the congregation, was an awesome experience. Surely God had a plan for the six-year-old little farm girl who joined the Fontanet United Brethren Church, was "saved" at fourteen at a church camp in Indianapolis, baptized at twenty four in the Raccoon Creek near Rosedale Indiana and at sixty served as an elder in the Loxa Presbyterian church. God truly has a plan and those who serve Him are amazed to be chosen or to have heard His voice when spoken to. Her heritage of being raised in a happy home with parents who taught her every day with their love and patience, and teachings of Bible stories and how to be applied to daily life, reflects in her story. She was capable of feeling the awesome love of God, the compassion of His Son, and the Holy Spirit that penetrated deep into her being. Her chest and heart physically felt the meaning of love. She knew how to love and how to be loved. Her prayers are for each one to hear the hymn, "Just As I am I Come," and to turn from any wicked way or thought, and experience the Love of God!

IT'S OK TO BRAG, ESPECIALLY FOR GRANDMAS!

The farm girl remembers her grandma Cox. She has fondest memories from about age six until age 12 before her grandma passed away. Six years of wonderful memories and ideals learned to stay with her a lifetime. Grandma made cookies that were always the same. None of her grandchildren will ever forget them because they were unlike any other. They were the size of a saucer and must have been a sugar cookie. A recipe that must have just been in her grandma's head....just a smidgeon of this and a dab of that and mix a spell. The more the grandchildren bragged on the cookies, the more cookies Grandma Cox made. The farm girl didn't realize until many years later that grandma loved all the grandchildren instead of just her. She thought she was the only one Grandma Cox bragged about. At Easter time it was a project to make a basket for grandma. She took color heavy paper and cut a square and then slashed the corners to be folded up and pasted. Her mother let her make paste out of flour and water. A strip of paper was attached to make the handle. The mom would help with boiling the eggs and she would use her favorite color crayons to make flowers and maybe even put To Grandma when she learned to write. After the grandma passed away and the family was settling affairs and sorting things at the home place, it was noticed that these little baskets were in the curved glass secretary desk. Grandma had severed the shell and eaten the egg and laid the shell back. That made the little farm girl proud to see grandma had saved her Easter baskets.

The grandma made a quilt top for her little farm girl granddaughter but didn't have it lined and quilted before she died. It was called the necktie pattern or some call it bowtie. Several years later the granddaughter contributed to the fund at the Fontanet United Brethren Church as she engaged the ladies aid to quilt it. It was displayed at the Coles County Fair a few years ago as an antique quilt with a story and won a Red Ribbon. The story went that the quilt top had been made for the exhibitor by her grandmother before 1938 and was lovingly quilted by dear old friends. The quilt had warmed the heart as well as the feet through the many years and will always be an heirloom of pleasant memories. Now a grandma herself, she wanted to share the story of the quilt.

Her grandpa Cox passed away when she was six years old and she has a few memories of him. Her Doty grandparents were dead before she was born. Stories related to her by her dad are treasured. Pictures and stories perpetuate her heritage. She realizes how important it is for asking questions and keeping written information for generations to come.

In the cemetery at Burnett Indiana she remembers the funeral of Grandma Cox. Hallowed ground of this well-kept country cemetery echoes the heritage and should be visited by generations to come. There are grave stones of Harvey and Laura Cox with deaths in the 1930s and a stone made by Harvey for their son, Herbert, who died at age 17. There is a daughter, Ethel who died in the mid 50s. In another plot is the farm girl's aunt Eva Cox Green and Uncle Jesse who are buried by their infant son, Bobby Eugene. Eva's son, Hurley, made grave markers for these loved ones.

Across the cemetery drive on the south side are her Doty grandparents, Zina and Dove Creal Doty. Other Doty aunts and uncles in this cemetery are Uncle Clay and Aunt Alma, Aunt Edna and Uncle Roscoe Haase. Her dad's brother Wallace and his wife Mindy, and her dad's sister Lena and husband Claude are other plots of the farm girl's kin.

In the far right corner of the cemetery are marble stones with names so weather worn and faded one can hardly read. They are stones of the farm girl's great and great greats. James Creal and Lewis Creal... Names implanted in genealogy and not to be forgotten although their stones have worn beyond being legible. Anytime is a wonderful time to visit cemeteries to reflect and especially on Memorial Day when tokens of our admiration are taken in the form of flowers to adorn the graves.

The now-grandma farm girl hopes to be remembered for how she might brag about her grandchildren, either verbally or within herself. She enjoys their antics and admires their maturity and talents. Her love is the same for each one. She was thrilled to spend time with Hollie and interact with her. Somehow it worked out on the Fourth of July that she could take her to the Parade in Mattoon. One year Hollie's grandpa wanted her to have a special dress. Being midway through summer most stores were displaying their fall merchandise with few summer things left. The grandma found one little dress she thought might do and then another one. The morning of the parade Hollie put on the first dress to show grandpa. His face displayed his disappointment that it wasn't what he had hoped for but he smiled and said, "Oh that is nice." He didn't know there was a second one. Hollie put on the other which was a dark pretty blue with red and white flowers and it had a bonnet to match. When grandpa saw this one, he beamed, "Oh now that is just what I thought it should be. You look like a little fire cracker!" At the parade many smiled and one older woman told Hollie she looked just like "Miss Fourth of July."

Hollie's mother discovered that she could read while she was very young. While being pushed in a stroller at My Store in Mattoon, her mother noticed Hollie was reading the labels on cans and boxes. She had learned while watching Sesame Street. The grandma had cousins, visiting from the state of Washington and Hollie was asked to read for them. Grandma wanted to show her off! The cousins were in a hurry to leave and a little kid's book was close by. That wouldn't work so the newspaper was given to her. She read an ad in the paper and made grandma quite proud when she said the clothing ad was for p-o-l-y-e-s-t-e-r. The cousin said, "Well I'll be – he wasn't sure he could have pronounced polyester, let alone a three-year old."

Hollie liked to ride in the front seat in a booster chair. It was fun for grandma to teach her the difference in a soybean and corn field. Driving along the Old State Road in rural Mattoon, grandma would make it exciting as she would quickly point to fields and ask Hollie, "What field is that?" She was amused at a quick reply, "Soybean, Grandma."

Hollie went to work with her grandma many times and the Student Life staff at Eastern Illinois University didn't mind at all. She did lots of errands and helped stuff envelopes and she learned to "type" the way her grandma taught her on the computer. It wasn't any wonder she chose EIU for college and she was employed in the office as a student worker. She had learned the office procedure including the Greek alphabet which helped her do the database for the sororities and fraternities. One thing Hollie's grandmother likes the best is her sweatshirt that says "Eastern Illinois University Grandparent."

Dane was another apple of grandpa's eye. At about age four he visited and grandpa had some treats for him. Dane said, "I like this sack of stuff and you Taylors are so good to me. Are you in competition with my other grandma and grandpa?" This was quite a grownup statement for such a little boy. He realized he was lucky to have Devereaux grandparents too! When he was older, Dane also visited his grandma in her office. He was there one time when 5000 flyers needed to be mailed out and he soon mastered putting the labels in just the right place and perfectly straight. He asked to go downstairs to the college bookstore and he used his own money to buy something for his grandma. She still has the EIU tee shirt magnet on her refrigerator. Dane was three months younger than Hollie and her birthday let her start school a year sooner.

One day when Dane's grandma Taylor was visiting his grandma Devereaux, someone said something about it being about time for Dane to start kindergarten. Noone realized how much he had heard talk about Hollie and her reading. He said, "Oh, heck I am not going to school. I can't even read yet." Grandma Taylor, realizing how much she might have been bragging, knew she had to bolster Dane's confidence. She said, "Dane, you don't have to know how to read to go to school. You will soon learn from your teacher. And just think what boys know that girls don't. You go fishing with your dad and you can put bait on your own fishing hook. And you can go to the woods and find mushrooms. And you can run real fast." Dane soon knew he was ready for school. Grandma learned that children take things very literal and she needed to be careful when and how she said things.

Dane has quite a resume. He has his credits at Indiana State University and his experience with jobs he has had since age twelve. His best friend's parents had a concession truck and he learned how to "do it all." He could flip a burger or operate the candy cotton machine. He worked several years at MCL Cafeteria in Terre Haute and left to work in a "kinfolk" owned restaurant, and other jobs of responsibility which was the youngest facilities manager in the USA for a grocery trucking company and an interesting job at Green Leaf, which is a small industry located in Fontanet, just down the road from his grandma Devereaux. Handy for him to drop by for a snack and to do any chores she might have.

Dane's grandmother Taylor was so proud to take him to her church one morning. He was about four and still could sit on her lap. The grandmother sang alto and thought she was pretty good and read the music to sing it according to note. And her voice was not a quiet one. She was singing away until Dane put his hand over her mouth and said, "Don't sing grandma, don't sing." Guess he thought alto was off key.

His grandma found a copy of a letter she wrote to him dated Holiday Season 1982:

Sixty Years in This Wicked World for Nuthin

"Dear Dane, 'Twas the morning after Christmas 1982,
and all thru Grandma and Grandpa Taylor's house,
Not a creature was stirring, Not even the dog George, or a mouse!
No snow on the ground,
And no sleigh could be found,
So some other way was needed
And no idea went unheeded.
A lad and his mom and dad had presents
And soon they were gone, in the truck to make known their presence.
Dane in his new November birthday p.j.s
To grandma and grandpa Taylor's they went
Dad drove the truck and knew the way.
The house in Mattoon was quiet and plain to see everyone was asleep.
The door was unlocked. They tiptoed in, passed Uncle Steve's bed
Down the hall that led
To grandma and grandpa's bed.
Grandpa sed, "Do you hear little feet
and a whispered hee hee? Can't be Santa Clause, no reindeer do
I hear.
Must be a sweet little boy
Who has come for a toy
Just then there was a clatter and Grandpa raised to see what's
the matter. And there was DANE with hugs and kisses
And Merry Christmas, We've come with Good Wishes!

Grandchild, Sheena, has her place special in Grandma's heart. When she was very young and small enough to lay on grandma's lap, grandma took her feet and bent her legs and taught her to "touch your nose with your toes." Much later as she was being screened to enter pre-school, the teacher was testing the three-year olds to perform various coordinating skills. The little ones were standing in a circle. When asked to "touch your nose." Sheena immediately dropped to the floor, slipped off her shoe, and put her toes to her nose! Her mother smiled but the teacher was perplexed until it was explained that this was a little "trick" learned a few years ago. It had been retained and memory triggered.

Time goes so quickly as grandmas get older. She could hardly believe it was Sheena as she answered the phone and hearing, "Grandma I need some college advice. Where do you think I should attend." "Will take some planning and discussion," and a nice conversation followed and phone call ended, "Grandma I love you.' Grandma said, "I love you too." May 28, 2004 grandma's heart swelled as Tasheena Jane Taylor received her high school diploma.

The grandmother still smiles when remembering Sheena when she was three years old. One morning at church, Sheena was dressed like a little doll. When the collection plate was passed, Sheena just smiled and reached in and took out a dollar. Grandma noticed of course, and didn't say anything. After the service Sheena was told, "Oh, Sheena, now you can take your dollar and put it in the collection plate. See the plate on the table up front." Sheena caught the enthusiasm of her grandmother, and looked so tiny as she stood on her tippy toes to put in the dollar. This was better than scolding or embarrassing an innocent child. And the grandmother told Sheena, "Next time we go to church, remind grandma to give you a dollar so you can put it in the plate when it is passed around." Sheena nodded that she would like that. This is a sweet memory and a happy one to remember.

HAPPY 16TH BIRTHDAY TO SHEENA
From Grandma Taylor
August 21, 2002..

Today is the day you celebrate
This most important birthdate.
would take all day for me to say
How much I love you in every way.
I'll just write a simple greeting for you
To let you know I'm interested in all you do.
I'm proud you are sweet as you are
And want you to aim as high as the brightest star!

Bridget was a brown eyed little baby beauty and just expanded her grandmother's capacity for love. One day she and Sheena were riding in the back of the car with Grandma. Bridget was happy and singing loud and clear the newest song Achy Breaky Heart. Grandma wasn't paying much attention until Sheena gave Bridget a reprimand. She said, "Bridget those are not the words!" Didn't stifle Bridget. She held her own with a retort, "They are my words!" Music was an interest as she was in drama, band and chorus and loved having grandma at school plays. Grandma thought back to high school days when she was in a class play and played the part of an old woman with powdered hair dressed in a gray pinstripe wool suit. She almost laughed out loud when she remembered one of her lines, "And I Ain't Lived Sixty Years in this Wicked World For Nuthin!" One day when Bridget was visiting her grandma, grandma couldn't find her cordless phone. She said, "Bridget, I want you to use your good eyes and find grandma's phone." Bridget looked at the phone base and said, "Grandma, all we have to do is push this button and the phone will ring." Sure enough they heard it ringing next to the chair in the living room. Her grandma would probably still be looking, if it hadn't been for Bridget being so up on modern things

ODE TO BRIDGET JEAN TAYLOR
"Hook Your Wagon To a Star"
May 30, 2002
From Grandma Taylor

Tonight there is excitement in the air
Hustle and bustle everywhere!
Graduation from 8th grade at Villa Grove
Hope the moon and stars shine from above!
When clouds do hide these heavenly lights
Clouds come and go and soon all will be right.

God made you special with plans for your life.
He will give you joy and lessen your strife!
You are loved by many who are with you tonight.
Keep Jesus in your life, Set your goals high,
Tune to God's plan as he watches from afar,
And Hook Your Wagon to Your Star!

The only way this Grandma Taylor could be more proud and would brag more, is to just have more grandchildren. Perhaps it isn't bragging but encouragement and recognition to applaud accomplishments and talents of these young ones. She looks at these dear ones and realizes how really strong they are but also fragile and recognizes their needs for loving guidance. She would hope her children would raise her grandchildren like she wishes she had raised her children. She would want her children and grandchildren to take any good points and build on them and improve in areas she may have been remiss.

Kinda out of the blue this grandmother was invited by her son's wife to go to Saint Louis to attend a series of Joyce Meyer Ministries evangelistic services. Her daughter in law had seen the programs on cable television. It would be good to spend some time with Jean. The two of them took off on a Thursday early afternoon for their motel in Saint Peter and then to the Family Arena in Saint Charles. It was an awesome spiritual experience which centered on getting to know Jesus and to know what God wants done. The instrumental music and professional voices ministered with rhythm and lyrics to stir emotions that opened hearts to receive the Words of God and accept Jesus as their Savior.

Saint Charles is a quaint little town along the Mississippi River. With its brick streets and its antique, craft and gift shops, it was like a hideaway to use some free time. They ate at the Lewis and Clark restaurant. Jean was toying with her soup spoon and once in awhile would look up and finally she asked, "Do you want to know a secret? Do you know what it might be?" Quick to wonder and even to surmise, the answer was, "Well, maybe. But until now I had given it no thought." She beamed and said, "I want you to tell me." And Jean grinned, "Yes, Tracy and I are having a baby." The reply to Jean, "You and Tracy will be wonderful parents. And I couldn't be happier!" Right there without any delay, the white haired grandmother felt her heart skip a beat as it stretched to include space for love for another grandchild. She knew there would be room for another!

These two were now better acquainted and knew they had several same likes. When Jean was quiet, she was asked, "Are you missing being home?" Jean replied, "Yes, and when you showed me some pictures of Tracy and Steve with their fish caught in the pond, I knew I would be glad to get back home. I haven't been away from him much." On the way home they talked about various things including how it was when Tracy was born and things he did as a child. And soon it would be his birthday. They talked about the many gifts Tracy hadn't taken out of the packages, including the watch two years ago at Christmas.

BIRTHDAY ODE TO TRACY
From mom

A 2004 birthday on February 5
This greeting will come as no surprise.
A present for you I would buy
But you've got unwrapped ones a mile high.

I couldn't find a card to say what I want to say.
It's also your great grandma Cox's birthday
who instilled in your Granny Doty, and she in me
Things hoped to have been passed on to thee.

Antics about you make a chapter of folklore
You're a pretty good son and if you'd listen more
I could soon have you perfect – a l m o s t
So share with Jean a Happy Birthday toast.....

Whether in a glass or with jelly

Time went fast from January until July 23, 2004. When Phone rang, and Tracy called his mother... and said, "Mom, Jean just checked in here on 2nd floor of hospital We don't think it is false. She hopes not." "OK, it is a little after 7 so should I go ahead to work in half an hour. I get off at 11:30 this morning." "Yeah, go ahead and after work you might want to stop by Jean's room 258." Sarah Bush Lincoln Health Center is located between Mattoon and Charleston. The grandmother-again-to-be lived only ¾ of a mile as the crow flies so it was handy to stop by. She soon found the room and surprised to see the door closed with sign "Mother and Baby are Bonding." A little knock and her son opened the door with a new daddy grin. The grandma was just in time to get a glimpse of the awake baby. Her little face with its fair skin and bright eyes and tiny nose would tug at anyone's heart. Her round head with its dark hair and her tiny fingers were truly a miracle just happened less than an hour before.

Joy truly does allow the heart to expand to make way for more love. Just as the grandmother knew, she could love another grandchild equally in its own unique corner in her heart. How blessed she felt for the new baby and to see the new mother and the proud father. Her prayers are answered and will continue for this family to be happy. Norma Mae Doty Taylor has a new granddaughter, Daisy Mae Taylor. Holding her for the first time was a special moment and she found herself cradling the baby tenderly and saying, "You're very special and pretty as a doll." And she stood and rocked her back and forth saying, "Do you want to swing and sway a little with grandma?" Daisy Mae seemed to enjoy it and grandma felt like she was dancing on air.

A Poem to Welcome Daisy Mae Taylor

On July 23, 2004, a pleasant day of summer weather
The Angels in Heaven got together
And God's creation to earthly parents released
A baby girl 7 lbs 14 ozs; no one could be more pleased.

Twenty inches of pure delight
With round face, skin so fair and eyes bright
Her fingers and perfect little feet
First prize winner of being dainty and sweet.

God chose Tracy and Jean to entrust for her care
They will love her and with others share.
Her family tree has so much to be proud
Relatives together are quite a crowd.

Genes make her unique – some from Lanphier
And Daily, Taylor and Doty to name a few.
Sisters Hollie, Sheena, and Bridget and Cousins
Aunts, Uncles all to nurture and keep her from fussin'

Grandmothers Daily and Taylor stand first in line
To hold and rock and to give, only when asked, advice
The Heavenly Father and the Angels decided the birthday
And will watch over the Taylor baby, Daisy Mae.

(by Grandma, Norma Mae Taylor)

ANOTHER TRIP FROM MATTOON TO THE FARM

A more recent roundtrip from Mattoon to the farm girl's home area stomping grounds... Early on a Sunday morning her phone rang it was her son, Steve. "Mom, do you want to go for a drive with us. Johnna and I want to go to see Linda and want you to go with us." "Sounds good to me, when are we leaving?" He said, "In about an hour." She said, "OK I will call Linda and let them know that her 'little' brother is coming over." She thought how good it would be. Steve and Johnna have a lot in common. They both love the songbirds and can name them. If one comes they don't know, they have a book for reference. They have many feeders and keep them filled. They have shrubs and trees with berries and bird houses. They can watch deer from their window in the woods. They have patches of wild flowers and appreciate the perennials and know which ones especially attract the gold finches, humming bird and berries for the orioles. If it is nature, they both enjoy. Two daughters, Jacena and Brittaney like to pick blackberries. Their grandma Taylor is real proud of them. They like being in the rural area with space to play with the cat, Tubby and dog, Lucy. They watch baby chickens grow up to hear the roosters crow and gather the good fresh brown eggs.

It was a cold day but sunny and not much traffic on I70, just a few trucks. About an hour's drive to his sister's. Steve's nephew, Dane, was there also and enjoyed some show and tell looking at the dogs, Opie and Briar, and hobby collections of shaving items, Captain Kangaroo memorabilia, crackle glass and International Harvester items. The six decided to "eat out" and went to an old neighborhood establishment in Seelyville. The food was wonderful and everybody ordered the sirloin steak combo with shrimp. Fun conversations made the event one to be remembered! Steve wanted to visit his brother in law's mother who lived not far. They drove past where his grandma Doty had lived and pointed out that he had built the fence. He told Johnna he had spent lots of time there. A little sad to drive by and realize so much had changed. The farm girl blinked back the tears as they drove by and she was glad the memories didn't change. There is still the shed her dad built out of railroad car door lumber. She felt young again as they drove on the road she had walked so often and she felt proud this was the house where she was born and still surrounded by fields and woods where she grew up.

They drove through Fontanet to show Johnna where the brick school used to be and past where the Bean Dinner is held each year. Eileen was surprised when they knocked on her back door. Steve asked if she remembered him and she said "Of course." She hugged him and was glad to meet Johnna. They visited briefly and managed to look out the window to see the many birds on feeders. As they left, Eileen hugged Steve's mother and said how much she loved her and how she loved her son's wife, Linda, and glad they share Dane as a grandchild.

Driving on the Rio Grande when they passed the Burnett Road, the farm girl remarked that the next time they came over, they should go to the Burnett Cemetery to pay respect to the farm girl's four grandparents. Harvey and Laura Cox and Zine and Dove Creal, Steve's great grandparents all in the same cemetery. Steve asked if it was Burnett where her grandfather built houses and asked the village hoodlums to watch the lumber and hired them to work for him. She said, "Yes."

Continuing on Indiana 150 as they drove through New Goshen, the conversation went to this being where the farm girl's grandfather had grown up. And they noticed all the stripped coal areas. David and Sarah Cox were his parents and they had come in an oxen cart from Virginia and probably settled there to work in the mines. Steve was asked if he remembered turning off the highway on a country road to Rosehill Cemetery where David and Sarah were buried. He kinda did and said some day he would like to go again.

The farm girl told the story how Harvey Cox who lived here in New Goshen area met his wife, Laura, who was born in Niles, Cook County, Chicago area. Laura had moved with her parents Levi and Helen Sparks to Saint Joseph Twp, Champaign County Illinois. Harvey was working on the railroad and Laura and her sisters were walking along the track. There were some boys who were bothering them. Harvey noticed and approached the boys to leave the girls alone. Laura admired Harvey's courage and respect for the girls. She set her cap for him and they were married in 1884. Steve laughed at the term "set her cap." Told his mother she should write all this down. She thought to herself, she may already have. And she gave deep thought of her son and how handsome he was driving the car and how much she appreciated him. She felt her heart warm at thinking how much respect she thought this son had for her. She admired that he was interested in his kinfolk of the past and how much he probably was like them, hard working, honest and a caring person.

Another one of many trips from Mattoon and the Indiana farm area and still too bad, there couldn't be a nickel for each mile so there would be many wealthy kinfolk! No nickels but no price is enough for "just another Sunday drive."

GOING THROUGH BIBLE

The now white haired farm girl often goes through her big Bible. She bought it while she still lived on the farm near Fontanet. She wanted to help her Uncle David who was selling Bibles and never realized how beautiful this book would become and how it would hold things most precious. Over the years newspaper clippings, cards and special paper items have been slipped in the pages and in no particular order. Often while she is relaxing she will reach for the Bible and open some pages. First she will see a birthday card sent to her from her mother and she is glad to have it in her mother's sweet handwriting. Under the nice verse is written "you are so sweet and good. Mother"

There is a browned paper with the words to a song she remembers being taught and she remembers the tune. She is so glad to have this hand written song on paper and still remembers her mother's voice.

Verse 1:   I am very happy, for I have a friend
           Who will always love me to the very end
Verse 2:   To God, now let me pray, He'll bless her every day
           My heart swells in pride, with happy memories stay

Chorus: Mother, dear mother. I love you,
           every day, every way. I'll be faithful true
           I'll never make you sorry or cause you anxious fear
           And someday you'll be proud of me, mother dear.

There is the application for marriage for her parents: Alice Cox to Grover L Doty dated 14 day April 1915 in

Vigo County Indiana. Also is the funeral memorial for her mother. Born October 22, 1892 died November 4 1981. Thomas Funeral Home in Twelve Points Terre Haute and buried in Roselawn Cemetery north of Terre Haute.

There is a satin bookmark that has the Beatitudes on it. Blessed are those who mourn for they shall be comforted...

And other scriptures she has embedded within her ..Ephesians 5:17-33 that is God's word for family and relationships. "Wherefore be ye not unwise, but understanding what the will of the Lord is. And be not drunk with wine, wherein is excess; but be filled with the Spirit; Speaking to yourselves in psalms, and hymns and spiritual songs, singing and making melody in your heart to the Lord; Giving thanks always for all things unto God and the Father in the name of our Lord Jesus Christ; Submitting yourselves one to another in the fear of God. Wives, submit yourselves unto your own husbands, as unto the Lord. For the husband is the head of the wife, even as Christ is the head of the church; and he is the savior of the body. Therefore as the church is subject unto Christ, so let the wives be to their own husbands in every thing. Husbands love your wives even as Christ also loved the church and gave himself for it. That he might sanctify and cleanse it with the washing of water by the word, That he might present it to himself a glorious church, not having spot, or wrinkle or any such thing; but that it should be holy and without blemish. So ought men to love their wives as their own bodies. He that loveth his wife loveth himself. ... For we are members of his body, of his flesh, and of his bones. For this cause shall a man leave his father and mother, and shall be joined unto his wife, and they two shall be one flesh...Nevertheless let everyone of you in particular so love his wife even as himself and the wife see that she reverence her husband. Chapter 6:1-4 Children, obey your parents in the Lord; for this is right. Honour thy father and mother, which is the first commandment with promise; That it may be well with thee, and thou mayest live long on the earth; And fathers, provoke not your children to wrath; but bring them up in the nurture and admonition of the Lord!"

With these Biblical passages and her dad's philosophy, she holds these truths to be the most possible meaningful. She feels very much at ease with the King James Version of the Bible.

In the Bible there is another funeral memorial with the picture of her Uncle David A Cox born April 12, 1900 died June 14 1982. Here is the memorial in the Bible he sold her. There is a Christmas card from him and Aunt Leona and she wrote a note: "we got your card and am glad you like your job. You said John now does the dishes. Tell him he does better than David because he just wipes them. Elsie will be here for Christmas. I will tell her to leave the gizzard alone so you can have it. HA HA. We saw your mother today at Mrs. Handlin's funeral. We are doing fine. With love." This probably was saved specially because when she was at her mother's for Christmas, she went down the road apiece to see Elsie and had a fun time and not knowing Elsie would become suddenly very ill and her funeral would be end of February. Elsie's mother, her Aunt Leona, was so genuinely grieved that it took its fatal toll. Not long after the Memorial Day Cox reunion she too passed away.

Turning more pages of the Bible, there is funeral memorial for her Aunt Eva Green born August 9, 1898 death July 1, 1966 with burial in Burnett Cemetery.

And a cousin, Lewis A Montague born October 18, 1912 died Feb 5 1991, buried Lower Mount Cemetery Covington Indiana. He was a son of her Aunt Flora. And there is a Christmas card from her Aunt Flora dated December 1963 with a note saying how she had enjoyed visiting in Mattoon and seeing the old windmill across the road. She liked good old fashioned things.

A funeral memorial for her Aunt Rosie, Rose Kardokus born December 7, 1893 died August 17 1962 and buried in Grandview Cemetery in Terre Haute. She remembers Aunt Rose for the warm macaroni and cheese and how good it felt to her aching throat after she had her tonsils out when she was six years old.

There is a letter dated March 12, 1976 from her Aunt Edith. It is a long letter but one part she likes is: "Now, I must tell you about your Uncle Emil. I believe I have told you about his rheumatoid arthritis. He did sleep with an electric blanket over him and an electric heating pad under him, but he still had so much pain and some nights had little sleep. Well, one of our friends sent a page of a magazine telling of a boy scout with arthritis who noticed he felt so good after sleeping in a sleeping bag. Others tried it and had the same results. Anyhow Emil has a sleeping bag and has no pain. Is fine of a morning. We know it helps and must be that body heat penetrates more than artificial. Our doctor laughed at him but we know it helps."

Her Aunt Edith's son, Gene, sent some thoughts the other day that she might slip in the Bible. His mother used to say when someone died, she called it, turning up one's toes and they never ate leftovers, they had scraps. When his mother was a little girl she would say she traipsed after her father, chattering all the time. The farm girl remembers too the verb traipsed. Gene wrote that once they were in Yellowstone Park. His dad parked by a small geyser, fortunately it was dormant. He walked over and put his head into it, inspecting it. His mother sat in the car, and in her usual quiet gentle way called, "Emil, get your head out of that geyser and come back to the car." They lived in Billings Montana and went to Yellowstone often.

Still reminiscing with the Bible, she smiled as she mused how her mother's sisters grew up and had their beaus and she is glad to have the ornate pressed heavy glass lamp that saw all the sparking. Her grandparents' lamp is on the dresser that her parents went to housekeeping with in 1915. These treasures are precious now in the white haired Indiana farm girl's rural Mattoon home. Hmmm, sparking, another word from the past.

The farm girl's Aunt Ethel is fondly remembered too. She remembers going to Gary Indiana for her evening funeral and then coming the next morning back to Burnett where she was buried in the six-grave plot with her parents Harvey and Laura Cox and her brother, Herbert, who died at age 17. The farm girl's mother mentioned to the minister that she would like for him to tell at the funeral how beautiful heaven must be. He did, and it made it easier for Alice to give up her sister. She had a son, Aaron, and a grandson, Paul. They lived with her Aunt Ethel and it was good that the farm girl could spend some time with them after the funeral from Thanksgiving to Christmas.

The farm girl was thrilled with television, that she didn't have at home in the mid 1950s and there were several Chicago stations to watch. The more she cooked, the more they bragged on her, so it was a fun circle. She helped her cousin sort through her Aunt Ethel's belongings, which to keep and some mementos for other loved ones. Paul was twelve and at the stage when most of the time he would stop at a cleared area about two blocks away to play before coming home from school. He would come in all sweaty and dirty and want to sit right down for a snack. To get him to wash up before supper was a chore. One day there was an early evening school dance. That morning he left instructions for a certain shirt to be laid out and that his pants be pressed. He wanted the bathroom to be cleared for him. He hurried home after school and wanted to know if his hair looked just right after his bath and was glad his clothes were laid out. The farm girl thought it was too bad there wasn't a dance every day. But also she was glad he could still be a little boy most of the time. Before she had left the farm, she had shopped and wrapped gifts for Christmas. She had helped Aaron shop too and they had packages to take back to the farm and put under the tree. While she was away her dad bought a television as a family gift. Christmas on the farm was a great experience for Aaron and Paul.

And it is hard to believe that her cousin's, Jean Sweet, obituary is in this Bible. She grew up with Jean and had so much fun going to the Indiana Roof and she was the one who encouraged her to someday write a book. Jean was raised in Burnett but not on a farm or she wouldn't have asked one day in an art class, "Do cows have tails?" Here is a poem that was written to her one Christmas to include with a stuffed plush cow wearing a red Santa Claus hat.

Sixty Years in This Wicked World for Nuthin

TO JEAN and all the Sweets----
From Norma Mae

Holiday Season 2000 is near
Glad Tidings to you I bear!
I looked for just the right card
But finding the right one, much too hard!

Tis time to get out the Christmas mail
Some will be email and some via postal snail
Will mail this early so will get there in time
And maybe it will fit your taste just fine.

I hope you like this card in the form of poem
And will keep it always in your home
When I saw this little cow so cute
I immediately thought of you

And take note; this little gift has a lil' tail
Will be easy to slip in the mail!
And sending card with this little token
Will save 33 cents, and that's no jokin'!

Merry Christmas to All and to all a Good Night
Hope the Holidays for you and yours are just Right!

Another funeral memory, not for her relative, but for the father of her son in law. Her grandson, Dane, is also the grandson of Deb and Eileen Devereaux. This memento reminds her when Dane was visiting and about 4 years old. He must have been greeted warmly and maybe given something along with the hugs and kisses. Dane said, "You folks are so good to me. Are you in competition with my other grandma and grandpa?" and such a big thought and grown up conversation for such a little boy. The memorial folder is for Harold "Deb"

Norma Mae Doty Taylor

Devereaux. He is the one in the class at Fontanet in 1928 that was taken by teacher, Orville Redenbacher, to the orchard of Dane's great great grandparents to trim the orchard trees. Typed on the bottom of the memorial is a poem that was read at the funeral, a little poem clipped from a magazine and most fitting.

> "I pray that I may live to fish
> Until my dying day
> And when it comes to my last cast
> I then must humbly pray
> When in the Lord's great landing net
> And peacefully asleep
> That in His mercy I be judged, Big enough to keep"

Very appropriate as a tribute to such a husband, father and grandfather and someone the farm girl knew when she was growing up.

Each time the big Bible is opened, she is taken back to Fond Memory Lane, often bringing a tear or smile and makes her love that Bible all the more.

SIXTY YEARS IN THIS WICKED WORLD FOR NUTHIN!

Each in their own way has a story to tell. A story is told whether it is written or remembered. To silence the truths that reveal what we think and why we think, is like Living in the World For Nuthin! For the one who played the character in the Junior class play portraying the woman of sixty years with white powdered hair, the words have echoed around and around in her head until this story is being written. If she only has knowledge of the present day, how would she know what to do without the experience of yesterday, and what would she do with tomorrow?

A story has been written from a character's line in a junior class play. The story meanders back from one era to another, from one generation to another, from one thought to another, from one coincidence to another, with each word and idea intermingled with logic, realism, dreams and in no particular order. As the story is written, so is life. Some of it may make good sense and some of it may not, some of it is funny and some is sad, some is understood and some not, some is relevant and some not. Life is perceived same as a story and it does not start and continue to the end in a straight line but does meander from one generation to another, from one incident to another, entwined with influence and teachings from others. Each incidence remembered is unique with experience of yesterdays, making people what they are today, and determines the degree of strength of faith for tomorrow.

God created a beautiful World and God created man in His own image to dwell in the world to have dominion over the birds and beasts. God created woman from man's rib that she should be a helpmate and they would produce children to populate the world. God gave man and woman a choice to live according to His Word or not. Some people make choices to do wicked deeds, and tragedies have occurred and will continue as a result. Others have made choices to live in this world to do good and to commune with God in prayer for their own inner strength, to appreciate their families, inspire students they teach, to honestly pursue their means for making a living, care and share with their neighbors, and worship sincerely in churches where they pray. The world is not wicked but there are those who are wicked in this world. God allows his created mankind the choice to say Yes or No, to be saved or not, accept or reject the Love of God.

Weaving and writing a story with only positive stories doesn't mean that there weren't failures, disappointments and discouragements. She made lots of plans that went awry and said many prayers seemingly made in vain that did not relieve her anxieties. She was discouraged when she thought she had a good plan and others were nonchalant and uncooperative. She regrets she passed opportunities to take a stand when she should have. She made mistakes, many she is aware and many not. She does believe that there is forgiveness daily when we ask and prayers are answered and not when or how we want. She believes if prayers aren't answered in one's lifetime, eventually without fail, God will respond!

Growing up on a farm attending the Fontanet school all of the twelve years.....Playing in school band and the Nevins Novelteers....Being in 4H...Working in Terre Haute and Mattoon and Charleston Illinois.....Belonging to the Fontanet United Brethren Church...Belonging and being an ordained elder in the Loxa Presbyterian Church.... Being married and raising a family...Member Number 701 in the Pilgrim Edward Doty Society, Inducted as an honorary member of the Order of Omega... A member of the Mattoon Homemakers Home Extension....Taking a 10 column Twentieth Century bookkeeping by hand to a completely computerized system for keeping books at an appliance television store and keeping statistical records for thousands of sorority and fraternity members, a member of AFSCME (the union Affiliation for State County Municipal Employees), Being a Stanley Home Products group leader and attending conventions in New Orleans, Las Vegas, Montreal, Nashville, Chicago, San Antonio....... Dabbling in antiques and collectibles and buying and selling on ebay .... have made quite an epitaph or story. It would take another sixty years for this farm girl to do all the things she has to do, things she wants to do, things she ought to do, and take time to do nothing.

The line in the Junior class play was, "And I Aint Lived Sixty Years In This Wicked World for Nuthin!"

The country farm girl in the 1945 Junior class play has a story written with influence from those who have touched her and with those she has touched. She knows what she believes and why she does. The portrayal of the old woman of sixty, impressed her as a young girl when she powdered her hair to play the part. Her story unfolded over sixty years as her hair turned to white. She looked beyond the wicked forces and the evils were not allowed to overshadow the beauty of God's World in which she lives.

Everyone has a story, whether written or remembered. The country girl whose hair has turned white through the decades, does not believe the World is Wicked. If she could, she would live on the little farm with her mother and father, be on the stage of the Fontanet school in the class play as a junior girl with long brown hair powdered and pulled in a knot. She would look at the audience to see her brother laughing. She would put her hand on her hip and point a finger. She would loudly belt out her line, "And I Ain't Lived Sixty Years in this Wicked World For Nuthin!"

Printed in the United States
31441LVS00005B/61-126